CLIVE ANDERSON
Our Man In...

CLIVE ANDERSON
Our Man In...

BBC BOOKS

This book is published to accompany the television series
Our Man In... which was produced for the BBC by Tiger Aspect
Productions Limited and first broadcast in 1995

Published by BBC Books, a division of BBC Enterprises Limited
Woodlands, 80 Wood Lane, London W12 OTT

First published 1995
© Clive Anderson 1995
The moral right of the author has been asserted

ISBN 0 563 37069 6

Set in Sabon by BBC Books
Printed and bound in Great Britain by Butler & Tanner Limited, Frome, Somerset
Colour separation by Radstock Reproductions Limited, Midsomer Norton
Jacket printed by Lawrence Allen Limited, Weston-super-Mare

PICTURE CREDITS

BBC Books would like to thank the following for providing photographs and for permission to reproduce copyright material. While every effort has been made to trace and acknowledge all copyright holders, we would like to apologise should there have been any errors or omissions.

BBC Books pages 3, 10, 11, 15, 19, 22, 23, 27, 30, 31, 34, 35, 38, 42, 43, 50, 51 (Colorific/ Dilip Mehta); 6, 54, 55, 59, 62-63, 68, 69, 72-73, 76, 77, 84 (Stephen Homer); 92, 93, 100, 101, 112, 113, 116 (Tom Owen-Edmunds); 128, 129, 132, 136, 140, 141, 144, 145, 152, 153, 156-157, 160, 162, 163 (Betty Press); 174-175, 182, 183, 186, 187 (Paul Harris); 203, 215, 218, 219, 226, 227, 230, 231, 234, 235 (Jim Buckley); **Gary Braasch** 195; **Russell England** 65, 89, 167, 178-179, 190, 191, 198, 199; **Geest plc** 97; **Hutchinson Library** 104 (J. Henderson); 121 (Philip Wolmuth); **Image Bank** 108-109 (James H Carmichael); **Images of Africa Photobank** 124, 148-149 (David Keith Jones); **Rex Features** 202 (Sipa); 211 (Jeff Jones); **Paul Sommers** 26, 39, 47, 105, 120, 125, 153, 210, 215 (bottom), 222-223; **Steve Terrill** 166.

CONTENTS

INTRODUCTION

THIS book is written to accompany the television series *Our Man In...*, for the purposes of which a film crew and I were dispatched by the BBC to six very beautiful places around the world to report on their problems. The series was going to be called *Trouble in Paradise* until it occurred to us that it might be difficult getting permission to film in some countries using a name which so obviously suggested things were not quite as wonderful as they seemed. Governments can be so sensitive. So *Our Man In...*, aptly enough, became our diplomatic title. It was not chosen just so the film about Cuba could be called *Our Man In Havana*.

Although all the films involved going to faraway places, they were not intended to be travelogues. We were supposed to examine serious issues, in more or less exotic locations, while having some fun along the way. We spent about two weeks in each country, most of which was spent interviewing key players in the situations we were looking at, or travelling to and from places relevant to our story. It is an unusual way to see a country. Filming allows you to meet a lot of interesting and important people, and those with strong opinions. But the work involved also prevents you from visiting many of the sights and scenes that most casual visitors regard as essential.

Deciding where to go proved more difficult than we had anticipated. We considered idyllic destinations from Nauru in the South Pacific to Harris in the Outer Hebrides. Unfortunately some places had to be rejected the more we researched them. Some were being covered in depth on news bulletins. Some seemed nice enough to visit, but you wouldn't want to film there. Some wouldn't let us film there anyway.

Finally we settled upon six paradises which were troubled, threatened or challenged by the modern world. Such is the way of modern life, it soon became clear that the effects of international tourism were going to crop up nearly everywhere we looked.

In Goa, India, it was the corrosive effect of tourism itself which was the subject of our film.

On the other hand, in the Maasai Mara, tourism, and the proper distribution of income derived from it, emerged as a possible solution to the threat posed to Kenya's wilderness and wildlife by the expansion of economic activity.

On the Caribbean island of Dominica, the absence of a substantial tourist industry contributed to a dangerous dependence on the banana trade.

Hawaii is of course very well known as a tourist destination and we touched upon tourism there too, though our film concentrated upon calls for Hawaiian independence from America.

In Cuba we looked at the problems facing Castro's bankrupt island paradise still Communist after all these years. Even there, the rich tourist raises his sunburned head as Cuba desperately seeks hard currency from luxury hotel development to sustain its egalitarian society.

Only in the Timberlands of Oregon, where we considered the fate of the ancient forests, was there no real tourist dimension to be explored.

Looking back on the places we visited, I fear we have been something of an angel of death. At any rate massive changes in each country seem to have occurred in the inevitable interval between filming the series and its transmission.

In Cuba we investigated the 35-year-old stand-off between Castro and America, only for the position there radically to alter more or less as soon as we got back to London. In Dominica there have been dramatic developments in the banana trade since we visited, none more so than a serious tropical storm which devasted the Windward Islands' crop. Oregon has had forest fires. And the outbreak of plague in India must have harmed the Goan tourist industry.

As I write these words I am listening to a news report of a tidal wave possibly heading towards Hawaii from an earthquake in Japan. I dare not look at any news from Kenya.

The genesis of the series was a slow one. I first started talking to a small production company called Aspect Film and Television about making some documentaries for the BBC several years ago. In fact I am not sure if the original idea was to do documentaries at all; things changed such a lot as we went along, it may all have started off as quiz shows. Anyway, my training as a lawyer does not help in these matters. I always want time to consider the next step forward, and I can always think of reasons to delay, to postpone, to adjourn *sine die*.

Probably I would still be holding things up, but the project fell onto whichever BBC desk Janet Street-Porter was occupying at the time. She suggested that I found out how I got on with documentaries in general and the distinguished director Mark Chapman in particular, by sending us off to Outer Mongolia by way of a railway journey from Hong Kong. This resulted in a *Great Railway Journey* on BBC television and a chapter in a BBC book of the same name.

I found the whole thing enjoyable enough to start making *Our Man In...* . Mark found the whole thing enjoyable enough to start making commercials instead.

The project was taken up by Mark's business partner, the equally distinguished Paul Sommers, and finally we set off to make the films. By now Aspect Film and Television had, by a process of merger and amalgamation, become part of the multimedia conglomerate Tiger Aspect Productions and Janet Street-Porter had been promoted to an ever grander BBC desk. (Now we have finished the films she has left the BBC altogether. I hope it was nothing I said.)

In contrast to making the documentaries, which is very much a group effort, writing the book has been a solitary activity. In the book I have tried to give the impression of the countries we visited, the issues which we were there to discuss, plus something of the process of filming as well. Although a book like this is conventionally described as 'accompanying' the television series, in this case, the better word would probably be 'amplifying'. There is only so much you can put in a forty minute film. So much more you can put in print.

The words and opinions in the book are all mine, but I have obviously drawn upon the research, planning and thought which went into the making of the TV series. Thus the book could not have been written without the tremendous work of the series producer and director of three of the films, Paul Sommers. Also involved throughout the project were Sam Anthony and Jeremy Lovering. They had several different job descriptions on the various films but between them they were responsible for producing the best ideas and the most interesting stories with a great deal of enthusiasm.

Many thanks also to Russell England who directed two of the films and to the several other excellent researchers, informers and fixers who accompanied and assisted me in the different parts of the world: Alison Aylen, Jeremy Gordon, Arlen Harris, Stephen McLaren, Ken Richards and Carolyn Roumeguere. And to Charles Brand for the lunches.

Since this is already reading like the first draft of an Oscar winner's speech I will refrain from thanking the marvellous camera crews and everyone else who worked on the series. But I must say how grateful I am to Sheila Ableman and Nicky Copeland at BBC Books for encouraging me to get this book written, almost on time, and for doing their best to make my prose readable.

Having said all that, I expect most people will buy the book for the photographs.

Our Man In...

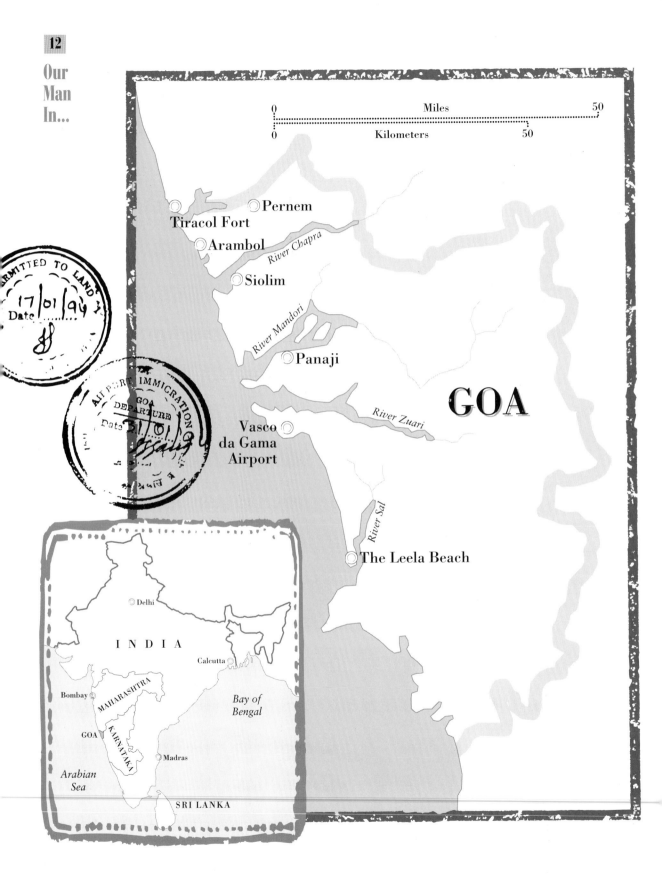

GOA

GOA is the smallest of the states which make up the Republic of India. It occupies a mere 1429 square miles (3701 square kilometres, if you want it in the metric system; one-fifth of the size of Wales, if you want it in Welsh). It is on India's west coast which, on a map, is on the left-hand side, an inch or two below Bombay. It is different from the rest of India largely because of its history.

The area was conquered by the Portuguese in about 1510 and it remained a Portuguese possession for more than four hundred years. Thus the Portuguese were in Goa a couple of centuries before the British began to establish their Empire in the rest of the subcontinent. And they were still there after India gained its independence from Britain in 1947. The languorous Portuguese rule continued until the Government of India 'reclaimed' Goa in 1961: impatient for a solution to the demands for decolonization, the Indian Army moved in and took over. The Portuguese had lacked the will to leave, but when it came to it they also lacked the determination to stay. But they certainly left their mark on Goa, chiefly by introducing Christianity.

India has never been exactly short of religions: firmly established within its borders are Hinduism, Muhammadanism, Sikhism, Buddhism and a variety of other isms and schisms. To the modern eye, it looks as though India has always had quite enough creeds to be getting on with. But in the sixteenth century the Portuguese felt there ought to be Christianity as well. With the high-mindedness and high-handedness of all European colonizers of the time, they set about converting the natives. And preaching the gospel of brotherly love was not then done in the milk-sop, clap-hands-come-to-Jesus style of today, but with a more red-blooded call to the faith, backed up with threats, violence, punishment and torture. It must have come as a shock: nobody expects the Portuguese Inquisition. Harsh methods, perhaps, but they worked. And today Goa still has a population of devout Roman Catholics.

For some time now they have been outnumbered within Goa by the Hindus who have migrated to this comparatively wealthy state, but it is the Christian tradition which sets this section of India apart. This is apparent not only in the white-walled baroque churches which are to be discovered in pretty well all the coastal towns and villages, but also in the lifestyle of the Goan people and their legal system.

I suppose that, in Europe, Roman Catholicism is not particularly associated with hedonism, nor with the emancipation of women. But in the context of Hindu and Muslim India, Catholic Goa has a more relaxed attitude to the pleasures of life – especially with regards to the availability and consumption of alcohol. And Catholic women have always been accorded greater property rights and are altogether less deferential to their menfolk than their Hindu and Muslim sisters.

So with its attractive beaches, available drink and free-thinking women, Goa has long been famous within India and without as the place to go for a good time. Some Goans profit from this, others rather resent it. Especially the women, who are naturally unhappy with the notion that because they look a man in the eye they must be making themselves sexually available to him. A notion which certainly seems to occur to lorry-loads of drunken young men who on holidays arrive from out of state.

In recent times, the first foreigners to put Goa on the map as a travel destination were what are still referred to in this part of the world as hippies. In the 60s and 70s, Goa was one of the great destinations at the end of the overland trail from Europe. Perhaps I should have come here then, hair down to my shoulders, beard down to my chest, drugged up to my eyeballs. Instead I went to law school. But I made it at last in 1994, even if most of my hair did not make it with me.

The hippies came from Europe to get away from it all, to discover Oriental religions, to live cheaply and to take drugs. Their arrival was not entirely problem-free. The introduction of a drug culture was resented by many local people, nude bathing by even more. But for the most part the hippies received a warm welcome from the people and the weather. They slept on the beach, survived on as little as possible and lived out the message of free love. For them Goa must really have seemed a paradise, which only had to be abandoned when their savings ran out, or the University term was about to start. All you needed was love. Plus, in the monsoon season, an umbrella.

But in the wake of the 'Beautiful People' of the 60s and 70s has come the mass tourism of the 80s and 90s. This involves building hotels, roads and restaurants and everything else the modern traveller requires to make him feel at home. In this there is far greater potential for making money, but also a greater potential for the destruction of the very paradise that people are seeking.

The growth of tourism is not a problem unique to Goa, but in many ways Goa is itself unique. I visited it to see how it was coping with the problems created by tourism. Was the way of life of the Goan people being destroyed by the arrival of foreigners looking for two weeks in the sun? Or did that represent a path to economic improvement? Did a few people

Arambol: the beach on a particularly crowded day.

staying in luxury 5-star hotels do more or less damage than larger groups of cut-price tourists? And was there any room left for the hippies?

To find out, I had to visit the beaches, go to the luxury hotels, seek out the beautiful and the exotic. It was a tough assignment, but somebody had to do it.

Advance to Goa

Since tourism was the subject of my visit, it was appropriate that I arrived in Goa by tourist charter flight direct from Gatwick. So much more convenient than a scheduled flight via Bombay, the producers assured me. Oh, and cheaper too.

The airport is not really an airport at all but an aerodrome operated by the Indian Navy. They allow package tourists to land there, but not scheduled passengers. Scheduled flights are presumably too much of a security risk. There is no photography or filming allowed in the terminal, for the same reason. So I had to be filmed later on, arriving in Goa by train.

Getting through the various airport entry procedures is not much fun anywhere, but in Goa the delicate balance between bureaucracy and chaos is a particular delight. Reaching the head of a queue to have piece of paper stamped by an official affords you no special relief as you immediately have to join another queue for a second official to check that the stamping has been done correctly by the first one. A system of checks and balances which keeps half the population employed and the other half waiting. This is, I think, typical of all India.

The hot and shabby arrivals hall gently simmers travellers' tempers, never quite bringing them to boiling point, as officials and clerks go about their business of stamping and docketing like nobody's business.

It is my special pleasure to arrive with a film crew, together with dozens of tin crates of film stock, cameras and other equipment. Who knows what amount of inspection and delay this might warrant? Earlier travellers to a foreign land would have employed a scout or guide to lead them across rivers and over mountain ranges. We modern-day television folk employed a man who came from Bombay simply to help us negotiate our way through the thickets of Indian officialdom.

Once past Passport Control, Customs and Excise, Baggage Reclaim and Visa Inspection, Goa was to be my introduction to India. And it was bound to be a pretty gentle one according to every Indian expert I spoke to in advance. Hardly any human misery or suffering to write home about. Oddly enough, this always sounded more of an apology than a reassurance. It was as though they were worried I might feel short-changed by the lack of typical experiences in the subcontinent, much as a visitor to England could be annoyed by the present-day absence of smog. Or a traveller touring the peaceful districts of America might be disappointed not to come across a genuine New York mugging or a real Los Angeles race riot.

Goa did turn out to be pretty, and mostly gentle, but there was quite enough human misery and poverty, thank you very much, for me to get the general idea.

Paradise found and lost

At first sight, Goa is certainly very beautiful. And at second and third, come to that. Washed by the warm waters of the Arabian Sea, its palm-fringed beaches look and sound for all the world like a holiday brochure. Inland, the countryside is more like an illustration from the *Jungle Book*. Forests and scrub land look wild and yet they are really quite densely populated. In amongst the trees are simple houses and shacks which are home to rather dusty, scruffy-looking men, whose wiry legs emerge from shorts or dhotis. All of them the living image of Spike Milligan in the Desert Campaign. In addition there are beautiful, dignified women, their slim bodies elegantly wrapped in spotless saris, patiently going about their tasks of washing clothes in the open air and cooking on pots over wood fires.

The roads are a hoot. For many years India has protected its car industry from outside competition. Its car makers have not, therefore, had to keep up with the advances made in Japan, or even Britain. So whatever was the rage on the road in 1947 is more or less still the rage now. Car parks look like a Morris Oxford Owners' Club Rally on a very sunny day in England. On closer inspection, the larger cars are called Ambassadors, an extremely good name for expensive, out of date, old warhorses which are only put on the road to maintain national prestige. Even more evoca-tive of a bygone British era are the Indian-produced Enfield motorbikes, which continue to be made to an ancient Royal Enfield design. And how weird to see the cows walking in and out of the traffic (a very Hindu side of Goa). Even weirder that it will only take a couple of days for this to seem completely normal.

In fact, for the first couple of days' filming I spent quite a long time on the roads, being driven around in a taxi by an extremely cheery driver called Ellias. He had five different horns which he used according to whether he was passing a lorry, warning a pedestrian, reversing or doing two other things not covered by the above. I think it is only in Britain that hooting at someone is unequivocally aggressive, its meaning ranging from 'Get out of my way' through to 'You are a complete idiot'. In most other countries it is usually no ruder than clearing one's throat to attract someone's attention. Here in Goa most of the lorries carry big signs which actually invite you to hoot when you come up behind them.

Driving conditions here generally feature that scary Third World combination of narrow roads, fast cars, overloaded lorries, bullock carts and people trying to stay alive while walking or cycling along the highway. Living a subsistence existence miles away from the big city grants you no immunity nowadays from the tyranny of the internal combustion engine.

More than once we came across someone lying in the road just out of the range of the passing traffic. It would be utter folly for us to stop and try to assist, Ellias insisted as he skirted round the body. It was probably a con man and not the victim of a traffic accident at all. Either way, to stop would be to invite a financial claim or being taken in for questioning by the police. Well, would we have stopped if we had knocked him down? Absolutely not, said Ellias, that would invite a financial claim, arrest by the police and being beaten to death by passers-by.

Where have all the hippies gone?

Calangute is my first port of call. Twenty years ago this was a little fishing village which became a famous hang-out for hippies. Now, the hippies are gone and most of the fishermen too. Today it is a lively seaside town with a collection of modestly priced hotels and boarding houses. The main street is lined with traders selling jewellery, blankets, souvenirs and knick-knacks. Is this the way the residents of Calangute make their money nowadays? Not quite. Most of the traders are from either Kashmir or Tibet. (There is political upheaval or war in both regions which has played havoc with the tourist trade at home.) Kashmiris are very insistent salesmen. Each one is offering a special bargain on the highest quality goods. Everyone has a brother round the corner who has even better stuff to sell. All are astonished if you pass by without looking, or look without buying, or buy something without buying something else. The Tibetans are more placid, sitting quietly behind their trays of jewels, much less inclined to haggle.

Calangute has a pleasant, rather than a spectacular beach, and an agreeable array of cafés and restaurants in which its visitors may refresh

Anjuna market, where hippies come to trade and traders come to be hip.

themselves. It is no longer a hippie paradise; it is not really a paradise at all, but it is perfectly congenial. It is neither cordoned off for the rich, nor trampled down by the masses. In many ways it is like a small English seaside resort, in the days when people went to small English seaside resorts for their annual holiday. I even bumped into a couple from Birmingham who explained they had been coming back to the same boarding house here each year, for several years. They hoped Goa would not get too popular and so get spoiled. I went off to the Planters restaurant for a lunch of kingfish and chips.

Ellias said that the hippies had moved further north, so I made my way up the coast to Anjuna market. This market was established years ago by the hippies themselves and it was sufficiently underground to be suppressed by the local authorities for a while. It is now back in full swing.

The market is by a beach, more or less in the middle of nowhere. The road to it takes you past little villages, corner shops and houses and empty fields, and past some signs to a German bakery which I never managed to visit. The market attracts large crowds who arrive on foot, on scooters, in large Ambassador taxis, smaller taxis of some other make (possibly Cultural Attachés?), or in mini-vans. The best way to arrive is on an Enfield. With your long hair, deep suntan, no helmet and a large bike thrumming between your legs you are forever in a real-life *Easy Rider* movie.

At the market we are all travellers, wanderers, beautiful people. Well, we are for the afternoon. Most of us are really tourists who are here to look at the beautiful people. Tourists may be driving the hippies away from here, but in the market the hippies are a tourist attraction.

Most of the stalls are the same as the ones you can find in Calangute or Panaji (Goa's capital). But there are enough spaced-out people in tie-dye shirts, girls with Janis Joplin hairstyles, shell-shocked victims of years on the road selling the contents of their backpacks to survive, to make the experience of underground culture seem real enough.

Alongside a highly organized leather goods salesman is a chancer selling half-empty bottles of sun cream gathered who-knows-how from sunbathers. A Scotsman in a kilt offers haircuts. All in all it is a fantastic ragbag of a place, a near-Bombay-mix of peasant market, Indian craft fair and Camden Lock, with a car-boot sale thrown in for good measure. It certainly takes me back to my youth because the Indian style of clothes and music was dead fashionable in England then. But I suppose it has always been fashionable here in India.

Most mysterious to me, although I am assured they are fairly common in India, are the ear-cleaners. Or, to be precise, certified ear-cleaners. One happened to approach while I was standing around – well, all right, posing – for a photograph to be taken for this book. In one hand he had a piece of paper on which somebody, possibly himself, had typed out that he was authorized to clean ears. He grabbed me by my right ear and, for the sake of a good photograph, I let him look into it ... No obligation to buy, he assured me. Just checking to see if I needed any remedial ear-cleaning work. But while I was getting instructions from the photographer, the cleaner scurried round behind me and, before I knew what he was doing, thrust what appeared to be a large rusty nail into my left ear. It was like having your windscreen washed at a traffic light, only painful.

Removing the nail from my ear, the ear-cleaner triumphantly displayed a large dollop of brown wax impaled on its point. Had that come from my ear, or was it on the nail from a previous client? Or was the whole thing a trick? Having a nail inserted into the ear struck me as a rather dangerous procedure, especially if the patient does not know that it is happening. Hey, there are even warnings on packets of cotton buds saying that on no account should they inserted into the ear. Surely they put the same warning on packets of nails in India? I began to speculate what nasty diseases I might have caught. Burst ear drum? Tetanus? Hearing Aids? Anyway, when he asked for payment, I turned a deaf ear.

Still clutching the side of my head, I bumped into two young English computer programmers who were travelling the world, on the proceeds of money earned from a few months' work in Hong Kong. Their earnings from programming computers meant they were able to spend many more months on the move. (Later in the year they were planning to go to a huge gathering at Macchu Piccu in South America.) Goa was great ... The only drawback came from riding around on locally hired scooters. There was no way of getting the right licence and insurance, so any policeman hoping to augment his meagre salary could always stop you when you were riding around and demand a bribe. He could ask for an even bigger one if you happened to be carrying hashish.

The computer programmers confirmed that the real centre of hippie activity, the way it used to be in Calangute, was further north, in Arambol.

The answer, my friend

The coast road winds its way north past Catholic churches and Hindu temples. Some of the houses are guarded by little model figures of soldiers, which is a Portuguese tradition.

The Portuguese language does not seem to have survived nearly as well as the models or the church. In fact, to my untutored ear, there was no

Anjuna market. ABOVE: *A certified ear-cleaner inserts a rusty nail in
my ear.* LEFT: *The beggar and the bargain hunter.*

Portuguese to be heard on the streets and none to be seen either: no signposts, no posters, no newspapers … I did try out one or two words of Portuguese of my own in Goa. Admittedly I remembered them from a couple of holidays in Portugal, but to say this produced nothing but blank looks would exaggerate the size of response I managed to achieve, even in people who had told me they still remembered Portuguese from their schooldays. Maybe it only comes back to them when they are doing quadratic equations.

And maybe it has not survived because the Goans have their own language to protect. It has been a struggle but the Goans have managed to retain Konkani, despite opposition to its use from Indian bureaucracy after independence, and centuries of severe suppression by the Portuguese before. It is still under pressure from the more widely spoken Marathi and, indeed, English. But there still exist Konkani books, Konkani schools and, for all I know, Konkani rhyming slang.

There is a river to cross, the Chapura, at a small town called Siolim. There is no bridge but an efficient ferry service carries about ten cars, plus as many motorbikes and foot passengers as can be crammed on. I chewed the fat with a couple of German motorcyclists. One of them had been bumming round the world for fifteen years. No wonder he looked like a disaffected youth of the 70s: he had been one.

Goa has several rivers like this and several ferries, but they are gradually being replaced by bridges. Bridges are grand things, things of beauty even. But a short ferry trip is a joy. Even for ten minutes it literally puts everybody in the same boat. Once a bridge is built, to the motorist it becomes just another stretch of road. The gain in time is minimal for the sacrifice in pleasure and interest. I dare say people said the same thing when bridges were being built across the Thames but, for an economy based on agriculture and tourism, speed is not everything. Anyway, we chugged across the muddy waters of the Chapura, waving to villagers splashing around doing their washing at the water's edge. It was absolute bliss. Another half-hour on the road on the other side and I was in absolute heaven.

Arambol village is a scattering of houses in the trees alongside Harmal beach. The beach is a huge stretch of sand, empty except for three or four fishing boats, basking in the sun and four or five refreshment shacks – *chai* shops, as they call them – stationed at the high-water line but not doing a roaring trade. In fact, not doing any trade at all.

So this was a beautiful, remote, uncommercialized stretch of coast. All the elements necessary for a hippie beach. But where were the hippies? Perhaps we had to wait for hippie hour.

Actually, the hippies were round the bend. A path round a headland leads to what is arguably an even more beautiful stretch of beach. It is certainly more remote. Out of sight of the village the New Age travellers, lotus eaters and sun seekers can strip off and dive naked either into the sea or the sweet water lake which is on the other side of the beach and fed by a freshwater stream which flows down a shady valley. It is not entirely a nudist beach, but drop out can become droop out and nobody will turn a hair.

Like a threatened, exotic species of life on earth, *Homo hippius* has been pushed to this northern end of his Goan range. Would I at last make contact with this fantastic breed, here in its natural habitat? Would I be able to talk to them? How could I break it to the hippies that the term 'hippie' has not been used seriously in Europe for about twenty years?

Actually I did make contact with Mike, who was originally from Switzerland. His lifestyle goes way beyond what anyone would usually call hippie. He lives in the trees next to the stream. His domain is a small platform of beaten cow dung. His worldly possessions are a hammock, a cooking pot, a flute and a catapult. The catapult serves no useful purpose, he only has it to aim stones at cans or tree trunks. He certainly does not use it to kill animals as he is strictly vegetarian. He has no books and no music except what he plays for himself on the flute. He does not appear to have any clothes; he certainly was not wearing any when I came with the camera crew to interview him. He sits naked in the woods, occasionally cooking himself a pot of beans. Back to basics, indeed.

His only vice, or indeed activity, was to smoke the occasional joint. Well, it might have been a frequent joint, come to think of it. The air in his clearing was quite intoxicating. I did not smoke, but I did inhale.

Mike has rejected the consumer society, Switzerland, Europe, the modern world and all its works. All of these he said were 'fucked'. I was not really able to establish anything much more specific than that. When I called on him he had a friend who was visiting from Germany. He was even quieter than Mike but was wearing clothes.

Mike's body was slim and healthy looking – perhaps we are supposed to live in the wild. His face looked quite old for his twenty-five years: perhaps smoking has an ageing effect, or Mike was troubled by his life back in civilization.

Strictly speaking, Mike was not getting away from it all. He, along with more or less everybody who comes to Goa to hang out in the great outdoors, goes back to Europe during the monsoon season which comes in the rainy months of June to September. Mike goes home to Switzerland to work for three months or so each year. He has very few outgoings (nothing on dry cleaning, for example). So he makes enough in three months in Switzerland to stay for nine months in India. In that sense he is really working for three months to take a very cheap nine-month long holiday and is perhaps not so different from someone who works for eleven-and-a-half months so they can take an expensive fortnight's holiday.

At any rate, Mike has found the lifestyle to suit him. In a remote corner of a forest in the back of beyond. Even so, it is not that easy to get away from it all. For the benefit of hermits like himself, hippies and unconventional travellers generally, boys from the village wander up and down this isolated valley with baskets of water melons and sandwiches, which they deliver to your hammock, cave or tree house, just like a City of London lunch service. Only cheaper.

ABOVE: *Back to basics. Mike from Switzerland amidst his worldly possessions.* RIGHT: *The sun sets over Arambol.*

Pig tales

Back at Arambol, I had a cup of tea in a little café halfway up a cliff over-looking Harmal beach. It was little more than a shack with a fantastic view, its kitchen equipped with hardly more than a Bunsen burner. But with these basic facilities, Peter, the owner, was able to produce elaborate and tasty meals (I stayed for dinner as well, which featured chicken, fish and prawns).

I wondered if there was a blot on his idyllic landscape. There is usually trouble in paradise.

Well, he had no trouble with the hippies. The villagers, Peter included, were devout Catholics and they had been offended by hippies bathing naked in front of their homes. But that had now stopped. Peter was not bothered by the hippies' lifestyle. The village as a whole were happy to augment their income by renting out rooms in their houses to budget travellers and running little cafés and bars which fell well short of over-whelming village life.

But yes, there was a cloud on the horizon. There were plans to build a luxury holiday resort practically on top of the village. The sweet water lake and Mike's green valley would become a feature in the grounds of at least one five-star hotel. Or become part of a golf course built for the use of rich Japanese golfers.

Wouldn't that bring prosperity to the village? I ventured.

Peter and his neighbour Philamena thought not. It would destroy the village. The hotels would take the land on which their cashew trees grow. The golf course would take the water from their wells. The beaches would be roped off for rich tourists. Large restaurants would take business from their little chai shops. Outsiders would take jobs as waiters. Village girls would become prostitutes ...

They were, in short, against it, and said so at length.

In fact they could have gone on all night about the horrors of the modern world being visited upon their way of life, but it was time to go to bed. Peter offered me a room in a house in the village.

The palm-thatched single-storey houses of the village are lined up somewhat randomly amongst scattered palm trees on muddy ground immediately bordering the sea. In addition to fishing, villagers earn their living by toddy-tapping. Toddy is the sap of the coconut palm. It is tapped by cutting into the trunk, in the same way that latex is gathered from a rubber tree. The only difference is that toddy is taken from the top of the tree. Morning and evening, the toddy-tappers shin up to the vertiginous tops of the trees with nothing but a loin cloth and a pot to tap into.

Toddy is highly prized in this part of India, though I must confess it was a bit too coconutty for my taste. I think it is better when it is fermented into a dangerous brew called fenny. This can be made from pure toddy, or mixed with cashew tree sap. Or, on occasion, adulterated with rougher alcoholic spirits.

While Peter led me along the muddy paths, past the water-filled ditches to my room, he introduced me to his father and brother who were going about their toddy-tapping business.

On his way to a room was a young chap from England, who was travelling through India with his girlfriend. They had had many an adventure staying in just these sort of places. He cheerily recalled waking up to find twenty rats around his bed in one village. On another occasion, he and his girlfriend had to protect their landlady from her drunken husband in the middle of the night. He was surprised I was staying in the room Peter had selected for me, as they had rejected it as not coming up to their minimum standard. Actually, the room was fine (bare, with a beaten earth floor), though the lavatory facilities were somewhat out of the ordinary. But what do you expect for forty rupees a night (less than one pound)?

To wash or go to the lavatory, I had to leave my room and walk 30 yards or so down a back alley. The shower was a simple cubicle equipped with a bucket which could be filled with water at the village pump. The lavatory was even more rudimentary, and much more unusual. It consisted of a hole in the ground, plus a pig.

'Pig toilets' are a feature of Goan life and they neatly do away with the need to have an elaborate sewage system because the pigs in Goa eat human waste products. Well, they may be human waste products to you, but they are meat and drink to Goan livestock. And to think I have heard people complain about bacon because they think they can detect in the taste that the pig was fed on fish … Ecologically sound this may be, but it is rather disconcerting to hear the excitement that your arrival in the lavatory excites amongst the herd of swine stationed strategically underneath. Do they ever get over-enthusiastic and bite the hand, as it were, that feeds them? Is it healthy? There are things like liver flukes whose life cycle would fit rather too readily into these sorts of conditions. Goan pork is regarded as a delicacy, but I decided that I am too delicate for such a delicacy and informed Peter that I did not want bacon for my breakfast.

And what sort life is it for the pig? Pigs have a famously well-developed sense of smell, and they are capable of nosing out a truffle growing several feet below the ground. I know they are often fed on swill, but here they were literally being shat upon from a short height. And, evidently, lapping it up.

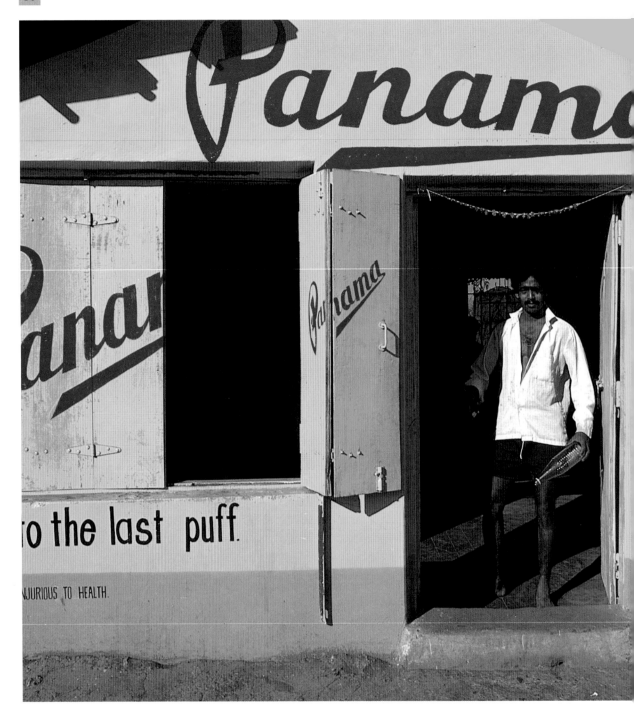

ABOVE: *Cigarettes 'good to the last puff'. Is it a slogan, is it a health warning?* RIGHT: *A toddy-tapper.*

In one of his *Hitchhikers' Guide to the Universe* books, Douglas Adams postulates a restaurant of the future in which diners worried about cruelty to animals are able to eat meat with a clear conscience. A special breed of cows has been developed which not only wants to be eaten but is able to speak to the diners to reassure them of that fact before they order.

I comforted myself with the notion that these pigs must be bred to it and happy in their work, even if they were not able to tell me so in person. In fact I did not give them a chance to get into conversation as I gave them a wide berth whenever I saw them wallowing in ditches or running around the village. After all, I did know where they had been. It was where I had been.

I wonder if Goan parents play with their children's toes. How would their rhyme go?

This little piggy went to market
This little piggy stays at home
This little piggy has human poo
This little piggy has none (lucky thing)
And this little piggy has wee-wee-wee, all the way home …

Mind you, this pig toilet business was not the comfort I am used to. I expect an en-suite bathroom. Next time I am in Arambol I shall demand a Gloucester Old Spot in my room. Or at least a potty and a guinea pig.

Fortified by a share of a bottle of Indian whisky, I settled into my room for the night to enjoy the simple life. Back to nature with nothing but my jungle-strength insect repellent, anti-malaria pills, a copy of *Madame Bovary*, and the BBC World Service on the radio.

The conditions in Arambol seemed medieval at first. Wattle and daub houses, livestock running in and out of everywhere, water drawn from a well. But I suppose country districts all over Britain were not so very different from this right up until the First World War.

Peace came dropping slow, there being nothing to disturb my sleep but the grunting of the pigs, the crowing of cocks, the barking of dogs and all the other noises that an inner city-dweller like me is not used to at night.

The next morning the film crew were on hand to record my waking up, washing and shaving. Naturally, they had not stayed the night in the village – there were no huts left for them. They had had to go off to find a hotel miles away, poor things.

It was not difficult to retain a very warm feeling for Arambol and its people, even in the cold light of dawn. As I shaved I mused that I was the man who so liked the village that he wanted to buy it.

In fact, that title might better belong to a German called Frankie. If he was a hippie it was in a very efficient, Teutonic sort of way. He dressed, always, in a crisp white cotton tennis shirt, of the type Franz Becanbauer might put on to play with his kids at the weekend. He did not wear his hair long any more because he had businesses in India and Germany, and he had to look respectable for meetings. But hippie or not, Franz – I mean, Frankie – had been spending half his time in Arambol for seventeen years and had put a lot of effort into preserving its charm and keeping it clean. It does have a litter problem.

Even people who regard themselves as travellers and not tourists and who want to fit in as much as possible with local people are not prepared to drink water from a well, thereby running the risk of contracting cholera and typhoid and other ethnic diseases of the lower gut. On a hot day they do not want to wait for a toddy-tapper to run up to the tree top for a bucket of coconut juice. They want a cold beer or a mineral water. The trouble is that these drinks come in bottles and tins. And a simple place like Arambol does not have an efficient waste disposal service. At least, not until they can breed a pig that likes to eat plastic, glass and aluminium. (I think the Pigasaurus in the *Flintstones* movie is a step in that direction.)

Frankie told me that he had taken it upon himself to clean up the beach, paying a couple of lads to pick up the bottles and other rubbish which had been spoiling this beauty spot. Although the beach was impressively clean, even with Frankie's help there were distressingly large amounts of plastic containers cluttering up the ditches and pathways around the village.

Frankie is spending money on Arambol, but the man who actually owns the place, and the man who wants to build a hotel development right next to it, is Jitendra Deshprabhu. So he was the man I went to see next.

Jitendra Deshprabhu lives in his family's country mansion just outside Pernem in the far north of Goa. Although they are a Hindu family, the Deshprabhus were always very chummy with the Portuguese rulers of Goa and were relied upon to protect Goa's border with Mathasdra. Their wealth and land holding has survived independence (there is no inheritance tax in India, I was assured) and Jitendra, as the current head of the family, is the owner of a vast estate encompassing something like twenty-seven villages.

From the outside, the mansion is an impressive if somewhat gloomy pile, its classic lines spoiled only by the extra bits of roof stuck on to the walls to deflect the monsoon rains.

Inside I am welcomed into a cool room, its blue glass windows and decor giving it a very Mediterranean (Portuguese, I suppose) feel. The

TOP: *Goa's beaches attract a mixture of tourists, locals and itinerant traders.* ABOVE: *Peter and I worry about the future of his bar.* LEFT: *The gorgeous clothes, jewellery and smiles of the beautiful women of Rajasthan and Karnataka are an attractive feature of the Goan scene.*

whole house is cool, kept that way by the airy courtyards. The number of courtyards is a sign of status. Someone doing quite well would be able to afford one courtyard to ventilate his home. Someone doing even better would have two; the Deshprabhu mansion has seventeen.

Elegantly dressed in a loose-fitting smock, he has the chubby look of the well-to-do in the Third World which shows they can afford to eat well. (As opposed to, say, rich Californians who are as thin as rakes showing they can afford private trainers, plastic surgery and low-calorie diets.)

Deshprabhu is amiable and aristocratic. He even has an imperial title. The pretender to the Portuguese throne recently invested him with the family's ancient title of Viscount of Pernem. Whether or not that counts for much in the Republic of India, he is certainly a Lord Bountiful. The school which is just outside his grounds was paid for by him and he is given to good works for the poor people who live on his land.

But why is he set upon destroying Arambol and its people with his hideous hotel development? While he answers this question he shows me around the mansion's guest annexe, which contains a few bedrooms, a gallery of portraits of his ancestors and a ballroom that would pass for an Oxbridge college hall.

He assured me that his ideas are not as bad as they have been painted. He is aiming to create a beautiful resort. This would bring wealth and prosperity both to him and to the people of Arambol. They would get jobs in the hotel, supplying food, driving taxis. He would not, as environmentalists claim, be depriving them of their drinking water. The huge amounts of water that 5-star hotel guests need to drink, bath in, see squirting out of fountains and to keep their golf courses green, would all be piped in from miles away. The golf course would not require chemical sprays, it would be fertilized by worm farms.

All this seemed a bit optimistic, and how was it to be paid for?

There were no golf courses in Goa. Surely it could support one or two? Did I know how much the average Japanese golfer spent on golf every year?

No, I didn't. The 4th Viscount had the figure to hand – £9000. With only a proportion of that multiplied by the many hotel rooms and condominiums available for golfers to hire, Desprabhu would be quids in. Aside from getting planning permission, all he has to do is get the millions of quids in as an investment and then he can get started.

The only ones really to lose out would be the hippies. 'Their' green valley, stream, and sweet water lake would become features of the resort. The hippies would be asked to leave, nicely. In any event, they just squatting on unused land.

He dismissed the opposition of local priests to the hotel development, claiming they resist change of any sort. They fear that any economic development would attract more non-Catholics into the state and break the priests' hold on the local people.

Let us pray

Arambol church stands a little way from the village, near the road from the south. It was built about one hundred years ago and is very pleasant, though it offers nothing special to attract the tourists – there are many finer examples of Portuguese colonial architecture in other parts of Goa. But it does attract the local people to its services. Three Masses are held here every Sunday morning, and they are all full. In fact, the church was extended recently to accommodate the congregation. Singing is done to the music of a guitar, lending a sort of Hawaiian lilt to the proceedings.

I thought Sunday would be a good day to find the local priests in the church and, indeed, Fathers Fernandez and Rodriguez were there conducting the service. They confirmed they were definitely against the hotel development. Father Rodriguez had been at a parish in another part of Goa where a similar hotel had been built. He had heard all the same claims about benefits to the local community, and the minimization of harm. But the community had been destroyed: jobs had not gone to locals and all the water had been diverted to the hotel.

The priests did not seem to be following a specifically Christian line on this. More a sort of anti-tourist revolution theology, inviting you to join their congregation in its struggle against unsympathetic development.

Most of all, they were against the golf course, showing me photos of a Japanese women's anti-golfing group which had visited them to show support. The priests, perhaps surprisingly, had no problems with the hippies, despite their (on the face of it) amoral lifestyle. Their only complaint had been the nudism, but that no longer took place in front of the village so hippies were all right. That was the Church's view. But what about the State?

For the official position on hotel development I went to the state capital, Panaji, and there sought out Mr U. D. Kamat, the Director of Tourism. Mr Kamat's office was in a rather shabby-looking building with the underspent, make-do-and-mend feel of government offices the world over.

Actually, that means it was not too bad, as a great deal of Goa appears to run on the principle of make-do-and-don't-mend. (I think this is true of all India.) It seems there is no power point in the country that does not

ABOVE: *Outside the church at Arambol.* LEFT: *Taking tea with Jitendra Deshprabhu in the ballroom of his house's guest annexe.*

hang off the wall; there is no wall which is not crumbling at the edges; no door which does not swing oddly from the wall. It is as though the place has been put together by one of those DIY enthusiasts who never has the right piece of equipment, and never quite finishes things off.

At two different hotels (admittedly neither were particularly expensive) I found showers equipped with an electric water-heater plugged into an ordinary wall socket. The socket was sited inside the actual shower cubicle, just inches away from the shower head where stray droplets of water were destined to come into contact, eventually, with the wires. Amazingly, I only received an electric shock once and that was because of a wholly separate electrical fault. I dread to think what Esther Rantzen would have said if she had been in the shower with me.

Anyway, Mr Kamat was good enough to see me. Unfortunately he was also good enough to see several other people before I reached the head of the queue. Worse, he was obliged to speak to a couple of dozen callers on the phone while I was trying to keep his undivided attention. Mr Kamat is a busy and important man in Goan tourism. Even when not talking on the phone he was signing documents. Bundles of them: letters, memos, chits … Who knows what? I hope he does because he had no time to read them. Evidently nothing can happen in his department without his signature. Equally obviously, there were far too many documents for him actually to apply his mind to the actions they were authorizing. A *Yes, Minister* world has arisen around him, and heaven knows how many others in this bureaucratic world, where the responsible person is too busy to be responsible for his actions. (A similar situation emerged at the highest levels of British government in the Scott Inquiry.)

When he was not otherwise engaged, Mr Kamat was very engaging and very enthusiastic about the prospects for tourism in Goa. Luxury 5-star tourism was the way forward. Hippies and backpackers do not bring in enough money. Package tourists might, but only if you allow in millions of them. International high-rollers bring in the money in low numbers. Mr Kamat was not worried that hotels would destroy Goa's coastline, forcing the international traveller to move on to some other Eden. It was true that the number of rich Germans coming to Goa had rather tailed off, but the arrival of vast numbers of British had more than made up for that. The Germans would be back once their recession was over. Strict controls were being enforced to stop buildings being too close to the beach and tourism was going to be the backbone of the Goan economy.

Mr Kamat suggested I visit the Leela Beach resort down towards the south of Goa. That is the future – he has seen it and it has the works.

Is your visit to Goa really necessary?

Before going south I went to Mapsa, a busy market town, to hear from the environmentalists who oppose tourist development.

Norma Alvires is a lawyer who runs the Goa Foundation. In her legal practice she regularly appears in court on behalf of the disadvantaged and oppressed. A sort of one-woman legal aid service. The Foundation publishes books and takes up environmental causes in opposition to the individuals and corporations who are out to make as much money as possible with little regard, as she sees it, for the environment.

Her immediate environment is unpretentious – you could say unpre-possessing. On the way to her office, which is in a block above a shop, I had to negotiate a path on which I came across a dead crow and a living cow which, although better than the other way round, are not what you expect to find on your way to see a lawyer. But then you could find yourself walking through a shanty town of homeless people these days in Lincoln's Inn Fields.

The arrangements in Mrs Alvires' outer office were reminiscent of an out-of-the-way shipping office in austerity Britain in about 1947. Two secretaries set about steadily sticking stamps on to packages and letters using a pot of glue and a brush: apparently Indian stamps do not come with adhesive. They have a computer but tend not to use it because of the frequent power cuts. (A couple interrupted our filming.)

In the inner office, sitting at a small wooden desk, Mrs Alvires is both charming and inspiring. She must make an impressive advocate. According to her, luxury hotels disrupt local life. They take water from the land so the water table drops and local agriculture suffers. If too much water is extracted, salt levels rise, killing agriculture possibly for ever. The local people do not always get the jobs it is claimed will be available to them. In any event, life as a waiter or cleaner is less dignified than farming the land. The price of food goes up. The hotels try to keep locals off the beach.

Not all of these objections would necessarily stand up in court, but together they sound like quite an indictment.

Mrs Alvires says the Indian legal system is basically sound, the judges are not corrupt and cases are generally given a fair hearing. As far as environmental worries are concerned, the government has put in place well-thought-out legislation. Regulations do exist to prevent hotels being built too close to the shoreline and to restrict the amount of water which can be extracted from underground supplies and so on. So that's all right, then?

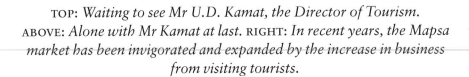

TOP: *Waiting to see Mr U.D. Kamat, the Director of Tourism.*
ABOVE: *Alone with Mr Kamat at last.* RIGHT: *In recent years, the Mapsa market has been invigorated and expanded by the increase in business from visiting tourists.*

Well, no. Rich developers tend to ignore regulations, break promises and generally act as though they are above the law. Politicians lack the political will to bring these powerful operators to book, so it is left to the Goa Foundation to take them to court. Operating as a sort of charitable, private environmental agency, the Foundation obtains judgments against hotels and the equivalent of prerogative orders to make government institutions intervene where the law says they should.

She says that although she opposes tourist development, the tourists who are here have reason to thank her. A tourist in search of paradise may want to stay in a hotel, but he does not want his view spoiled by lots of other hotels.

The Goa Foundation is not the most militant of environmental activists. That title might belong to the Goan Vigilante Force (GVF) which is the IRA to the Goa Foundation's Sinn Fein. (Actually that is not really accurate. The two organizations are not connected, and they do not blow people up, but with any luck you will see what I mean, and they will not sue me.)

Ronan Martin is a leading light in the GVF, and he was about to demonstrate in Mapsa against the tourists who have in recent years invigorated Mapsa market, so I went there to see him. Once a strictly local affair for the selling of fish, fruit and vegetables, the market now attracts stalls selling the clothes, jewellery, baskets, bags and carpets that tourists feel they have to buy to prove they have been to Goa. Many of the stall-holders had also been at Anjuna.

While waiting to film in the market I had my shoes shined. Well, 'shined' might be putting a bit of a gloss on the procedure. I had the dirt on them moved around a bit. Whatever you call it, it was a thoroughly depressing experience.

If you hang around long enough in India, say two seconds at the outside, you will be approached by somebody offering to sell you something, asking for assistance, or begging for money. Bear in mind I was in Goa where this sort of thing is at a minimum. Strolling around the market is enervating for an uptight Englishman like myself. If only the stall-holder would stop offering me stuff I might be able to find something I wanted to buy. If you do not buy anything, salesmen and women crowd after you. If you have not bought yet, they want to make a sale, and if you do buy something they all crowd round you, reckoning that if you have bought once you will be prepared to buy again.

It is much the same with beggars. They hold their babies, they expose their wounds, they tug at your sleeve. Have you a heart of stone? Have you any change left? Give to one, why not give to all? I am a sucker for the beautiful mothers with placid children strapped to their backs, but everyone here looks in desperate need.

Gypsies from Rajasthan and Karnataka have an excellent technique. Whether selling clothes and bags decorated with mirrors, or simply begging, their pitch is to come and sit with you patiently until you hand over some money.

Locals working with us dismiss all these people. They are itinerant nuisances. Not Goans at all. Their husbands all have well-paid jobs. They are professional beggars. Perhaps they are, but they and their long-suffering children seem to earn their money just the same.

While all this was going on, the shoe-shine boys tugged at my feet. I am about to appear on-camera, and my shoes are covered in the red mud of India. I have money in my pocket. I am waiting anyway. I am the perfect customer and I agree to the shoe-shine. The boy asks for fifteen rupees. I haggle. Eventually I beat him down to fifteen rupees. I learn later that I am a mug, I should have beaten him down to five rupees (about ten pence). He wants to take my shoes away to do a proper job. This I do not allow. I am not that much of a mug.

He takes out what might be described, quite accurately, as an empty tin of shoe polish and, with his nail finds some vestige of Cherry Blossom still adhering to the thread in the lid. He uses his fingers to smear this on my shoe and then buffs it off with a moth-eaten piece of brush. The whole exercise leaves my shoes no cleaner than when they started. It is a perfect example of the free market not working in India. The price of a shoe-shine is too low, but he cannot charge more because a thousand other street urchins are there waiting to undercut him. But at the going rate he cannot afford to buy any polish. If he got paid more, the shoe-shine would cost more, but at least my shoes would be shined. And he would be able to make a living wage. As it is, he has gained hardly anything, and I nothing at all.

While I was standing in the market (fighting off the subsequent offers of shoe-shines – reasonably enough, nobody believed I had just had mine done), another modest area of reform came to mind. Street-sweepers in Goa are usually small women bent nearly double using brooms made out of bundles of sticks. I guess the street-sweepers are untouchables or, at any rate, people trapped in low-paid work. But their bundles of sticks are not that good at sweeping up litter, and neither are the sweepers. They swat limply at the rubbish on the street like teenagers set do some task around the house. They cannot refuse to perform, but will not bring themselves to do it with anything that could be mistaken for enthusiasm. Before a pile of rubbish has been formed or put into a bag, it has mostly blown away again, or been kicked along the street. All right, buy some proper brooms. It would cost a little more, but at least the streets would be swept.

Higher wages might help the work rate as well. The sun must be affecting my brain. A few days in India and I'm turning into a Communist.

Ronan Martin wants to turn me into an activist. Or at any rate stop me being a tourist. About four of his army parade around near the market with very well-made signs telling foreign visitors of the damage that our presence brings along with our travellers' cheques.

He insisted that the golf courses with their holiday villages, financed by Japan, would essentially amount to the Japanese exporting their old age pensioners. He would not allow that 'tourist farming', as I wanted to call it, was an acceptable use of natural resources. He would not even countenance the idea that a golf course constructed on waste, barren land could not be, well … constructive.

In the eyes of the protesters, the tourist industry simply could not win. If they build on farmland they are taking land away from agriculture, but if they build on barren land they are doing something unnatural to the environment; if they spend a lot of money they raise local prices, but if they pay low wages, they exploit local people.

Playing around

And what about the golfers? The threatened construction of golf courses seems to excite more ire than virtually any other proposal of the tourist industry. My conscience is clear on this; it is not a game I have ever taken to or been any good at.

On hearing this, the director of the documentary decided to make me play a round of golf with General De Silva. He has retired from the Indian Army and become involved in the public debate about golf in Goa. The idea was that I should interview General De Silva about golf while I was shown making a pig's ear of the game myself.

We played on a small course that General De Silva designed himself. It is part of a luxury Taj hotel development on the coast. This features all the things that the Goan Vigilante Force dislike: restaurants near the beach, green lawns, swimming pools, exclusive beach. I had to force myself to try them out and hate myself for enjoying them all.

On the golf course – not much more than a pitch and putt – and on-camera, General De Silva said he thought it was ridiculous the way golf was being linked with prostitution and drug-taking as a great evil. It was a pleasurable game and Goa and India could do with some courses. True, it was being introduced to Indians by foreigners, but that had been so with

Playing a round of golf at the Taj hotel.

cricket, and nobody thought that cricket grounds should be removed because they were alien influences. He had criticisms, too, for the tourist industry. He felt developers were being greedy in hurrying to build expensive golf courses for the benefit of, or the exploitation of, wealthy Japanese people. Courses should be established for local people first. Only that way would a course develop a character which would eventually attract outsiders.

All in all, he was the most agreeable and reasonable person I spoke to about this issue.

Naturally, the General's interview is not in the documentary. Apart from anything else, and by a peculiar operation of sod's law, instead of looking an idiot on the golf course, my shots went annoyingly right. I drove the ball down the fairway, I putted in from 12 feet away from the hole. I could have been, well, if not Nick Faldo, at least Jimmy Tarbuck. Then the film ran out and I reverted to my usual level of golfing ability – slicing, hooking and missing with the worst of them.

Leela Beach

According to Ronan Martin, the villain of the tourist piece is Captain Nair, the developer of the Leela Beach. And yet the Leela Beach hotel complex is, according to the Director of Tourism, the very best the Goan tourist industry has to offer. It is some creation. On the coast at Colva Bay, it has 250 luxury hotel rooms surrounded by freshwater lagoons, walls and uniformed guards.

The main buildings are pink. Their architectural style is Suffolk farm-house, teamed with Portuguese Colonial, with just a touch of Disney. In the way of these islands of luxury the design is way over the top, but nothing like as tasteless as a nearby resort which is built in the shape of a Portuguese galleon. It has all the trappings of the luxury tourist hotel, the swimming pools, gymnasium, restaurants. You can choose from Indian, Goan, Chinese and international menus. There are a few tacky examples of poor finishing off, such as stucco walls coming unstuck, but in the main it achieves the effect of leisured opulence.

The guests seem more or less contented. The less contented ones complain about the slow service. One couple had waited an hour for a drink at the poolside. It is all very well being in a Third World country, but they wanted first class service. But another man approached me in the gents to say he found everything absolutely fabulous. And it's a long time since that has happened to me.

It is difficult to tell when they are stripped down to their Lycra swimwear, but these people do not appear to be the filthy-rich independent jet-setters which the travel industry cannot get enough of. Most of the guests seem just like package tourists who everyone agrees it is possible to have too many of. Of course, there are shops within the complex so there is no need for those tiresome shopping trips into the real world. Once here there is no reason to leave.

A sign at the beach advises guests not to eat from stalls and shacks outside the boundaries of the hotel, but promises a 24-hour medical service for those who do. Local people are not completely forgotten, however, as there is a garden decorated with cardboard cut-outs of village houses and village people. They have displays of Goan life in the evenings, but unfortunately I did not get to see it as I was out meeting real Goans in a real Goan village.

Captain Nair is, I think, a self-made man. He certainly made a fortune from textiles and looks as if he is doing all right from the hotel trade. In conjunction with Lufthansa he operates the Leela Kempinski Hotel in Bombay which, by all accounts (not just his), is a magnificent international venue. And the Leela Beach is his next success. He put in sixty per cent of the capital for this venture himself.

Sitting on his private balcony overlooking the lagoon (there are villas and flats available on the site) he is proud of the hotel complex. He has created a garden paradise here, with trees and water and everything, where once there was 'sand, mere sand'. Regulations which prevent him building too close to the shoreline are tiresome nuisances to be overcome like any other problem.

Captain Nair is dismissive of environmental objections generally. He gets water for the hotel by tapping the immense monsoon rainfall which otherwise would run away into the sea and be wasted. He has no time for the notion of leaving Goa as a wilderness. He has the confidence of a wealthy man who is well-connected. Virtually every minister in the Indian government has been to his hotel to enjoy his hospitality.

To say that he was bullish about the future of the Indian tourist industry would not quite capture his obvious enthusiasm. Buffalo-ish might do it.

He said that new free enterprise policies are being followed in India. These, he claims, will have ten times the effect on India that Margaret Thatcher had in Britain. So it is not the time to sign up as a coal miner in the foothills of the Himalayas.

By the time I interviewed Captain Nair I had visited the Goan village just outside the boundary of the hotel complex. My guide to the way

Protesters draw attention to the long term damage that hotel development can do.

things were on the other side of the tracks was Michael, who runs the improbably named:

A corner of Italy 'Yes That's
VENICE BAR AND RESTAURANT'

There was nothing particularly Italian about Michael's bar. It was a shack that sold beer and served local food. It was one of the few forlorn buildings which formed what was recognizably the same sort of village as the charming Arambol in the north. Except that now it was overlooked by the staff quarters of the hotel. The wall marking the boundary of the hotel seemed to squeeze against the village as though trying to push it into the creek. Barbed-wire fences restricted the villagers' access to groves of coconut trees and the beach. One or two houses in the village were fenced off completely. In short, it had lost its charm. In fact, it was more like visiting a concentration camp.

The villagers here and in Arambol enjoy certain rights as tenants, or *munkars* as they are known. They have a hereditary right to stay in their houses, as long as they can establish good title. This usually requires some written document. Official pieces of paper carry great weight in Indian legal bureaucracy. Although they do not own the trees as such, each *munkar* has the right to tap specific coconut trees for toddy, and may have similar rights to make use of cashew nut trees. In English law, this would be like an easement or profit *a prendre,* under which people in an area are entitled to cut wood or graze animals on the lord of the manor's land.

The problem for Captain Nair and other modernizers is that *munkars* are difficult to get rid of. Some can be bought off, but most wish to stick to their traditional way of life. They realize that a sum of money is soon spent, whereas their rights to a house and trees can, in theory, last forever.

The problem for the *munkars* is that they lack the money to stand up for all their rights, and are powerless to prevent the character of their neighbourhood being destroyed around them.

Looking around the now charmless village the unworthy thought does cross one's mind that a lot of effort is being expended to make life here as unpleasant as possible in order to drive the *munkars* away. With the help of Ronan Martin, a charge had even been brought against Captain Nair that he personally had attempted physically to intimidate a woman called Annie whose house was right next to the hotel.

After dark I was taken round the village by Michael. Right in the middle of the collection of flimsy houses was a pumping station. The pump was leaking or overflowing. And sewage was oozing into the ground, leaving a quite revolting stench hanging in the tropical air.

Rich people's sewage escaping right next to poor people's homes. The unacceptable faeces of capitalism. Outside the house, which was practically next door to the pump, no more than 20 feet away, sat an old man, taking the air, and coughing his guts up.

When I interviewed him, Captain Nair would not accept the evidence of my own eyes and nose. Sewage was used to fertilize the coconut palms, he maintained. They had the best disposal system money could buy. He certainly had done nothing to intimidate Annie, who in the past had worked for him. He was expecting to rehouse her once a financial settlement had been reached. The idea that he, friend of the powerful, should be convicted of a criminal offence was obviously quite incredible. I suppose, on this point, he must be right.

The real problem is not Captain Nair. He is just someone trying to make an honest few million bucks. The problems come from the clash between the rich, modern world of tourism and the uncomplicated lifestyle of the folk who have lived in idyllic simplicity for generations. My sympathy was very much with the Goans struggling to hang on to their paradise, but let's face it, my lifestyle is that of the developers and their customers.

That 'each man kills the thing he loves' is certainly true of the tourist. We are all looking for the virgin country we can deflower, the unspoiled beach, so that we can be the people to spoil it. The best time to visit any tourist destination is always ten years before you actually get there. Ten years ago the fishing village still had fishermen, and the local bar still had locals. Now, it is full of people like us.

Tourism, someone told me, is now the biggest industry in the world. Rich cities like New York and countries like Britain and Italy depend upon it. It would be quite remarkable if a beautiful but poor tropical state like Goa were to resist the temptation to sell itself to the tourist.

Obviously, making a TV programme and writing a book about a place like Goa, even though they focus on the problems of tourism, is likely to attract more people there than it repels.

So I am part of the problem and not the solution. But perhaps this is not somewhere to visit for a holiday. It might be better to choose a destination which has a less fragile culture to be destroyed. In fact, nothing of any real worth at all. Somewhere like Eurodisney. After all, Eurodisney needs the money even more than Goa.

Our Man In...

CUBA has an unhappy history. Columbus came across it in 1492 and the Spanish thereafter set about conquering the island and eliminating its Indian population. This process was so successful that other Latin Americans claim to be able to identify Cubans by their complete lack of Native American blood. Resistance to the Conquistadors was led by an unusually warlike leader called Hatuey. But after a few months he was captured and burnt at the stake for his pains. He now lives on as the brand-name of a popular Cuban beer: when the heat is really on, have a cool Hatuey.

Cuba's wealth developed on the back of the tobacco and sugar trade and on the backs of the slaves imported from Africa by the Spaniards. Emancipation of slaves was a long time coming to Cuba. There were major uprisings from 1868 onwards, but slavery was not finally abolished until 1880.

Independence from Spain came in 1899. The fight against Spanish domination was supported by the Americans, but this led to half a century of domination by America. In fact it first led to the Spanish-American War in 1898, a conflict sparked by the sinking of an American battleship, USS *Maine*, in the Bay of Havana, combined with the encouragement of tycoon William Randolph Hearst who reckoned that a war would help to sell his newspapers. The idea! It is as though in our times the Gulf War had been waged for commercial interests, or American troops had landed in Somalia for the benefit of TV cameras. As luck would have it, the Spanish-American War led to America acquiring the Philippines, Puerto Rico and other Spanish colonies. It's an ill wind.

America did not gain formal jurisdiction over Cuba but, with the Spaniards gone, American capital was invested heavily in the island, American businessmen controlled its trade and American politicians exerted an overwhelming influence on its general development.

A succession of scarcely democratic governments failed to cope with Cuba's economic problems in the first half of the twentieth century until the military dictator Sergeant, later General, Batista took control in 1952. Under his rule Cuban life was the heady mixture of oppression, corruption, exploitation and prostitution captured in Graham Greene's novel which he set on the island and which, by coincidence, he also called *Our Man in Havana.*

Fidel Castro attempted to overthrow the ruthless Batista regime in 1953 when he was only twenty-five. He was captured but, being perhaps not quite ruthless enough, the regime decided to exile rather than execute him. He returned with Che Guevara and eighty other guerrillas in 1956. At one stage Castro's forces were reduced to only twelve but in 1959, with relatively little blood spilt, he finally pulled off a somewhat improbable victory with a combination of skill, charm, determination and good fortune. His luck, if that is what it is, has stayed with him ever since and kept him in control for thirty-five years.

Few ordinary Cubans were sorry to see the back of the Batista regime but Castro's land reforms and appropriation of property hit the rich and affected American economic interests. By seizing their assets he put Americans' backs up and their noses out of joint.

Whether Castro's rule began as a Communist revolution is a moot point. From the word go, Castro was committed to redistributing wealth, but it can be argued that it was only the complete hostility of America that pushed Castro into the arms of the Soviet Union, which was delighted to get a toehold in America's backyard. Castro's revolutionary slogan was changed from *Liberty or Death* to *Socialism or Death*. As a battle-cry, *Socialism or Death* is an inspiring turn of phrase. But after thirty-five years in government, it sounds awfully like a threat.

The idea of a small island, even if it is the largest in the Caribbean, with a population of only 10 million, being able to insist on following a strict Communist line a mere 90 miles away from Miami is, for the rest of the world, a rather amusing joke, albeit one which does have a serious side. For instance, the Soviet Union's attempt to site nuclear missiles in Cuba in 1962, and President Kennedy's reluctance to let that happen, nearly led to a nuclear holocaust. If that had happened, nobody would have remembered where they were when Kennedy died because we would all have died with him.

For thirty-five years America has refused to trade with Cuba; the Soviet bloc which used to trade a great deal with Cuba, and subsidize its economy, is no more; and yet Castro still soldiers on.

So can he be counted as a success? Well, staying in Cuba is certainly one measure of success. But many of his fellow Cubans do not choose to stay there with him. Every year, hundreds of them take to the sea in anything which might keep afloat for 90 miles to escape Castro's socialist paradise. For many it is socialism or death by drowning.

You have to go to Cuba to find out what it is really like. It is impossible to get a clear idea by talking to other people about it. Opinions on Castro and Cuba are polarized in the extreme. Before I went to Cuba I spoke to lots of Cuban Americans. There are more than a million and a half in Miami alone, most of whom seemed to be gathered for their

In Cuba I always had the feeling that someone was looking over me.

annual street party, 'Calle Ocho' in 8th Street on 12 March. None of them had a good word for Cuba as it is today. I tried to tempt one of the most affable of their number, a budding politician called Joe Garcia, into saying something – anything good about Castro. He declined. It was, he said, like inviting a Jew to say something good about Hitler.

Well, I suggested, Benito Mussolini at least got the credit for making the trains run on time. Was there nothing like that?

Nothing.

I reminded him that Castro is widely credited with improving literacy rates, building hospitals and schools. Infant mortality rates are amongst the lowest in the world … Joe was having none of that. Far from being an economic disaster area, when Castro took over Cuba it was out-performing everyone else in the area. Of course there have been improvements in social services since then, but there have been advances everywhere and they are not always accompanied by Cuba's human rights abuses.

In print it is very much the same story. Jorge Mas Canosa, Chairman of the Cuban American National Foundation, writing in 1993 compared Cubans in America with Cubans in Cuba:

A spiritually and materially prosperous nation in exile, and an enslaved, destitute, hopeless nation on the island.

On the other hand, Mary Murray, a journalist who has lived in and written extensively about Cuba, interviewed the Cuban Foreign Minister, Ricardo Alaracón, in 1992. The interview was published in a pamphlet, and included this exchange:

Q How is democracy working in Cuba?
A It works better than in the United States. It could work even better than it currently does. We're working on improving it.

Could they be talking about the same place?

Take me to Cuba!

Since America imposes a complete trade boycott with Cuba you might think it would be difficult to fly there from Miami without hijacking an internal flight at the point of a gun. In fact, it is quite easy. America forbids anyone to make money out of Cuba, and certainly does not want Cubans (of the Castro persuasion) making money out of America. So it will not let a Cuban airline fly into the States, but it will allow an American airline fly to Cuba. You get on the flight to Havana by queuing up a few hours before take-off, in good time to have your luggage weighed very carefully. The aircraft cannot cope with suitcases loaded with too many items that are unavailable in Cuba.

The American government only allows its citizens into Cuba on journalistic assignments, and the Cuban government does not like to let many of its citizens go to and from the States, so I rather hoped the plane might be half-empty, but it was full of people paying a visit to their relations in Cuba. One or two were dressed up in several hats and extra layers of clothing, not because it was cold but so they could beat the luggage weight restrictions.

Miami is amongst the most built-up of American cities, rivalling Los Angeles for freeways and skyscrapers and urban sprawl. Everything in Miami is big, flashy and new. Everything in Havana is very different.

On arrival in Cuba the roads are attractively traffic-free. Great to visit, though you might not want to drive there. Here and there are magnificent gas-guzzling American automobiles of the 50s, fantastic machines built just before Detroit went completely space-age crazy with fins and wings. I had been told about these cars before I got there and in fact there were not quite as many as I was expecting. Once the revolution happened the American car-dealers ran out of stock or ran out of town. I suppose I imagined that the street scene would be 1959 America trapped by a Vesuvius of economic sanctions. The truth is that while there are still quite a few automobiles which would not look out of place in an early series of *I Love Lucy*, most of them must have fallen to bits some time in the last thirty-five years. In many ways it is surprising that any remain at all. The survivors could all command a huge price on the international vintage car market, even with the DIY additions and bolt-ons which their enterprising owners have had to resort to over the years to keep them on the road.

The other vehicles on the roads are mostly Ladas. Lada cars, stretch Ladas, Lada taxis. Taken and driven away, no doubt, by Lada louts.

There are almost as many overcrowded buses. Plus lorries and some tractors which are pressed into service to provide public transport. More serious even than the shortage of vehicles is the shortage of fuel to run them on. Everyone has to leave work quite early in the afternoon because just queuing for a bus takes three hours or more for most commuters.

OVERLEAF: *Cuba, where American cars are built to last. 1950s gas-guzzlers keep going despite the shortage of parts – and gas. Buildings show their age too. Even the windows are overwrought.*

To alleviate this problem, an ingenious ruling requires that all government-provided cars stop for hitch-hikers. This ordinance is no dead letter. There are special people at street corners to hail the passing civil servant, minister or official, and to organize the hitch-hikers into orderly queues. This is a system we could well adopt in Britain. Virginia Bottomley, say, on her way to close down another hospital would have to share her Ministerial Rover with a few patients from the waiting list who are waiting at the bus stop and a couple of nurses who are trying to get to work.

We started our look at Havana in *Plaza de la Revolución* – Revolution Square. Revolutionaries like squares. Moscow has its Red Square, Beijing has Tiananmen Square. Even in London, any decent march or demonstration has to go to Trafalgar Square (apart from that 60s anti-Vietnam demo which took place in Grosvenor Square).

This square is a bit bleak. It is large, tarmacked rather than paved and, apart from a monument to Cuba's national hero, José Martí, completely featureless. The buildings which surround it are 50s Stalinist and dull. The front of one, though, is dominated by a massive outline of Che Guevara. I think it is the Ministry of the Interior, though it could be a giant Athena poster shop.

Che Guevara had the right idea. The James Dean of radicals and hero of the revolution, he did not hang around getting old and unpopular in power. After a few years in government in Cuba he went off to join another revolution, this time in Bolivia where he died a martyr's death. Age cannot not weary his radical chic nor his good looks. A glamorous politically correct icon, he remains forever – a cross between Tony Benn and Hugh Grant. Not bad for an asthmatic Argentinian medical student with an allergy to mosquito bites.

Failing to find inspiration in the square, I checked into my hotel, the Sevilla. This was the Seville Biltmore in Graham Greene's *Our Man in Havana*, which was written just before the revolution. Since then the hotel has spent several years in decline but now it has been restored to something of its former glory.

It has eight floors of rooms and three restaurants. On the ground floor is a cool bar in an open-air courtyard. The staff are extremely friendly although the service can be slow. On the ninth floor there is a high-class restaurant in which they have got almost everything right for

A magnificent figure dominates the largely empty Plaza de la Revolución *(plus me in the foreground).*

the international diner. You know the sort of thing: there is a plate laid in front of you which is taken away once you have ordered your meal, to be replaced by the plate your food actually comes on; a phalanx of different-sized glasses; lots of waiters with excellent command of English to guide you through the menu and congratulate you on your choice. Everything a high-class restaurant should have, only the food is not particularly good.

Downstairs there is an informal buffet in which the food is largely inedible, though it served a pretty good breakfast which was even popular with a large party of French holiday-makers.

Graham Greene said that the Spanish made much more of an effort to build magnificent cities in their Caribbean possessions, comparing the ramshackle townships of the British West Indies with the flamboyant architecture of proper cities like Havana. I do not know what Graham Greene would make of Havana today. Most of the Spanish Colonial buildings he knew are still standing. No, that is not true. Most of them are falling down. Some have fallen down already. Here and there are what look like bombsites. They are the remains of elegant apartment blocks, or whatever, which have collapsed under the accumulation of years of neglect. Some surviving, elegant facades are held up with crude wooden supports; other buildings manfully stay upright against the odds, subdivided as many times as possible into flats for the citizens of Havana.

The view from my hotel room is astonishing. A few years ago the Americans started to develop the neutron bomb, which was going to kill all the people in a battle but leave the buildings standing. This city looks as though it has been hit by a bomb with the reverse effect. Perhaps it would be a proton bomb. No people have been killed but the fabric of the place has been completely destroyed. I have never been to Beirut but after years of civil war it cannot look very different from this.

I found the sight of a city crumbling around its inhabitants profoundly depressing and also quite inexplicable. The explanations everyone gives for this mess are that, after the revolution, the priority was to build hospitals and schools in the country, not to titivate the capital city … And they are short of hard currency … And then there is the American blockade … None of which quite accounts for thirty-five years' lack of routine maintenance, however worthy the other aims of the regime might be. UNESCO has apparently stepped in. My guidebook tells me they are doing painstaking restoration work in an attempt to save something from the wreckage. Just next door to the hotel is a good example of a magnificent, delicately decorated building being well-maintained and put to good use. The Cento Provincial de Entreramento was built as a fencing school, and is now used mainly for gymnastics. There are two floors of long galleries linked by winding stone staircases. Everyone trains here, from the smallest school children to Cuba's highly successful Olympic-champion gymnasts.

The long airy galleries are ideal for setting up parallel bars, or doing floor exercises. Even the flights of stairs provide excellent indoor training runs for the children. Using a beautiful building, once available only to a privileged élite, for the benefit of the highly successful national sports effort is a symbol of what might have been achieved.

The building opens out on to the Prado (or the Paseo de Martí, as it is officially called). The Prado is a famous city street which has a paved promenade down its centre. In Batista's day it must been a great place to walk, to be watched by secret policemen, and to get hassled by prostitutes and cigar-sellers. Nowadays it is a great place to walk, to be watched by secret policemen, and to get hassled by prostitutes and cigar-sellers.

The Malecón is an even more famous highway, a wide road which sweeps around Havana's waterfront. Here the buildings seem to have fared particularly badly. Perhaps if Cuba was still under American influence the buildings would have gone by now anyway, replaced by high-rise hotel developments or at any rate obliterated by advertisements for McDonald's hamburgers – the disagreeable facets of capitalism. Crumbling buildings, though, make very poor advertisements for Communism.

If the buildings were in a much worse state than I had expected, at first sight the people on the street seemed much better. Cuban Americans had warned me that, cut off from good food, cosmetics and the high life, Cuban Cubans walked around with gloomy faces, poor skin and shabby clothes. In fact Cuba retains a very vivacious atmosphere. Everyone walks around dressed as sexily as possible, the men admiring the girls in their Lycra shorts or revealing dresses. It is all a bit macho in a Latin American way, but at any rate not gloomy. A country of crumbling buildings and beautiful women. Which is, I suppose, better than the other way round.

But it does not require a much closer look to realize that life is actually pretty grim for the average Cuban. The average Cuban queues up not only to get on a bus, but also to buy goods in a shop, when they are available. Basic foodstuffs are rationed. Shops for the average Cuban are dreary counters where your allowance of rice and cooking oil is doled out to you. In one shop I went into, only one product was displayed on the shelves – tins of dull-looking beans. I commiserated with the shopkeeper. It was a shame that was all she had to sell. Actually, she

ABOVE: *The Hotel Sevilla. Some buildings in central Havana have been restored for the benefit of foreign tourists.* RIGHT: *The Cento Provincial de Entreramento makes good use of the former fencing school. The orange blur is a young student exercising on the stairs, the red blur is me.*

explained, things were worse than that. The tins were empty. They were just there for decoration.

In contrast to the average Cuban, the above-average Cuban, or at any rate the unusual Cuban, can do better. In Cuba if you want to buy luxury items like fashionable clothes, or soap or toothpaste, you have to have hard currency. And 'hard currency' means American dollars. Such is its global power that the American dollar rushes in even where Americans fear to tread. And it does mean that factory workers, doctors, even government officials, struggle to eke out an existence on Cuban pesos, while more and more Cubans turn to prostitution, taxi-driving and selling cigars on the street to foreign tourists. One black-market taxi-driver we spoke to had, only a year before, been one of Havana's most successful businessmen, but he had been driven to taxi-driving by the need to make money that can actually buy something.

It was time to start filming some of this and time, therefore, to make contact with our government minder. His name was Raphael Padilla, Press Attaché at the Ministry of Foreign Affairs. A really jolly good sort, Raphael's mastery of English idiom, ancient and modern, suggested he must have been attached to Cuba's London Embassy since early childhood. In fact he has never been to England, so is a walking tribute to the Cuban education system. He was very bright and breezy, loyal to the regime and anxious to do everything to assist our filming except appear on-camera himself. He did provide a translator/guide for this purpose, a forceful Jamaican woman called Louisa who years before had made her home in Cuba.

The first interview Raphael arranged for us was with Carlos Azugurray, a high-ranking government official: the Advisor to the Foreign Minister on Global Affairs. I met him in the magnificent Foreign Office Building. Foreign Offices always have the best premises, they are the best parlours that all governments keep to impress visitors. This building was a rich man's folly which had been built in the 30s and then donated to the nation.

Mr Azugurray's English was very good as well, though more formal than Raphael's, at least in the setting of a televized interview. With him I essayed some criticism of Cuba's condition. He agreed that economically they were in a bad way, but not in terminal decline. The way forward was still with socialist principles, despite the collapse of the Soviet Empire in Eastern Europe.

But what about the shortage of food, the lack of transport, the collapsing buildings?

Well, that was the Americans' fault for not trading with them.

We got into an interesting discussion about political prisoners. I had yet to speak to any opponents of the regime, but it is the Cubans' human rights record by which, above all, the Americans justify their economic sanctions. There are supposed to be thousands of arrests, hundreds of political prisoners.

The Advisor assured me that Cuba did not have hundreds of political prisoners. When pressed for a figure he suggested that fifty political prisoners might be about it. He stoutly maintained there was freedom of expression – the only thing which was discouraged was support for America – and Cuba most certainly was a democracy.

Wait a minute, democracies usually have different parties, and governments are voted in and out of office. Fidel Castro was President for Life.

No, the Advisor maintained that Cuba was a democracy, even though it was not readily recognized as such by other democracies. Castro is a great man. Not that there was anything like a cult of personality.

Take me to your leader

Well, whether he was a cult or not, Castro was the personality I wanted to meet or, at any rate, see in the flesh. And as chance would have it there was a possibility for me to do just that. Recently there had been rumours that Castro might be ill or even dead. It has to be said that there are more of these rumours than there are political prisoners in Cuba's gaols, but there was going to be a big opportunity for Fidel to appear in front of the world's media to show he was still alive.

A shipment of goods was to be landed that day at Mariel Harbour by a group of people called Pastors for Peace. This was a group of American clerics who, appalled by their own government's policy of cutting off supplies of American food and drugs and other essentials, were prepared to break the embargo as a gesture of goodwill. Castro himself had turned up to receive the first boat-load of goods, and he was rumoured to be doing so again today.

We hurried over to Mariel Harbour, which is about an hour's drive from Havana. The trouble with Castro is that he is often scheduled to be at a certain place but then simply does not turn up. Actually, 'scheduled'

OVERLEAF: *Old Havana is a city of crumbling buildings and beautiful women. Better than the other way round?*

is the wrong word. Rumours just circulate that he is going to make an appearance, so I suppose he cannot be criticized when the story turns out to be false. Whether the fact that he makes very few public appearances is due to pressure of work, a security measure or because he suffers from Alzheimer's disease is anybody's guess, or prejudice.

The omens were reasonably good at Mariel Harbour. There was enough checking of press accreditation and fussing around by security staff to suggest they really were expecting the great man. There were plenty of news-cameras and reporters. The Reuters reporter was fairly certain Castro would not wish to pass up the chance for excellent publicity. The *Morning Star's* man in Havana agreed.

The Pastors for Peace boat was tied up to the harbour. On board was a yellow school bus and a variety of other necessities. I would imagine a shipload, though impressive, would be little more than a token gesture but the Pastors were well received by the crowd. A very orderly crowd, mainly school children, stood maybe fifty deep along the dockside while the arriving Pastors glad-handed the front rows and received their cheers like political candidates on a walkabout.

The Pastors were an eclectic mixture of religious worthies, the American equivalent of Hampstead intellectuals, student activists and aid workers. A middle-aged lady assured me that her neighbours all thought it was marvellous that she was coming on this trip. Perhaps she was one of the ones from Hampstead.

The excitement built as the speeches began. The Pastors were led by the Rev. Lucius Walker – the new Dr Martin Luther King, according to a sympathetic member of the Press corps. He addressed the crowd in English and his speech was simultaneously translated into Spanish by one of the several people standing on the platform. The line of them up there facing an open-air crowd made the whole thing feel like a proper old-style political rally.

The Rev. Walker's speech started well. He berated America for maintaining a blockade of Cuba, pointing out that America sees itself as the land of the free. He went on to praise the great work that Cubans were doing here, and to call for the assistance of God in promoting the work that had brought him and the boat here. His speech kept reaching a climax and then starting up again, a tactic by which we were teased along for an hour-and-a-half of rhetoric, bombast and oratory. Was this his usual style, or was he just playing for time? Had Castro been delayed?

The speech degenerated into telling us the ages of the people on the boat (youngest twelve, oldest eighty-six, if I remember correctly). The climaxes got weaker and weaker and finally we came to an anti-climax: the realization that Castro was not going to make an appearance after all.

The Press corps sensed this and started to drift away. Enthusiasts in the crowd hung on ready to cheer Fidel's famous bearded face. In the end any beard would have done. We would have cheered David Bellamy. Or anyone with particularly heavy designer stubble.

Ordinary people

No luck with the leader, but Raphael was able to set up an interview with some ordinary people. Well, fairly ordinary. Francis is the president of his housing block's CDR – Committee for the Defence of the Revolution. He is in his sixties and lives with his wife in Calle Obispo. Their flat is fairly typical for central Havana. Entered via a gloomy staircase, its high-ceilinged rooms have been divided horizontally to create bedrooms above the living room. Perhaps the strain of these subdivisions has contributed to the collapse of so many buildings over the years.

Francis and his wife are enthusiasts for the revolution and are anxious that we show exactly how bad things are in Cuba, to demonstrate the evil effects of the American boycott.

Although I had some idea of what a CDR was I had assumed it was rather like a Neighbourhood Watch scheme: a small group of community-minded locals keen to do their bit. No, Francis told me, everybody in the block is a member of the committee, except one old woman who is slightly too long in the tooth. And they all report to each other about counter-revolutionary behaviour, which they generally sort out amongst themselves. Only with very serious matters, usually people coming in from other districts, do they have to involve the police. Working through my official translator I never managed to get him to explain what he meant exactly by counter-revolutionary behaviour or counter-revolutionary elements. One abstract expression was always explained by reference to another.

These committees could be seen as the basis of Cuban democracy. Or the basis of all-pervasive social and political control.

What I could see in the shops was certainly further evidence of the desperate conditions of the people. No one appears to be starving, but there is practically nothing for sale. Francis's wife took me to a local store. It was arranged like an indoor market, but the goods on offer would have been left behind at a lacklustre car-boot sale. An old man cheered things up with a tune on his guitar as we inspected a strange selection of bicycle pedals, plastic jewellery and plastic flowers.

ABOVE: *At the moment there is not much in store for the average Cuban and queuing has become a way of life.* RIGHT: *A typical weather-beaten ruin.*

Notwithstanding the views of Cuban Americans, Cuba has a very high international reputation for its medical service, but its pharmacies have no drugs. Francis took me to his local chemist's. It is very picturesque with interesting bottles on wooden shelves, an old-fashioned apothecary's. But it has nothing to dispense. Nothing behind the counter except the staff, who continue to work there despite having nothing to do.

Since it was the end of the afternoon we decided to call in at the Café Paris which is not far from Francis's home. This is a lively, trendy place which serves tourists, plus the Cubans who can afford its prices. We had been here before for lunch, which was fine. This afternoon, though, they had run out of coffee and tea. Forced, then, to have a beer, we sat as boys approached us from the other side of the lattice-work windows begging for chewing gum, or cash. 'One dollar' is the street cry of Old Havana. Tourists often hand out pens so the boys even demanded the biro I was using to write up my notes.

And a packet of Embassies

The next day we experimented with travelling around Havana in something other than a taxi. Buses seemed rather slow so we eventually came up with the idea of hiring a motorbike. Apart from the police, who have Italian machines, motorcyclists in Cuba make do with rather clumpy Russian bikes, usually with a sidecar. I assured Louisa I was a competent motorcyclist and she sat in the side car urging me to slow down as I fought to move the bike's clumsy gearshift. We managed a tour past the extraordinary edifice which houses the Russian Embassy – it looks rather like an airport control tower. Some people say that, now the Russian presence has been scaled down, the building is going to be converted into a hotel and conference centre. But then some people said Castro was going to be at Mariel Harbour.

While Louisa recovered from the experience of riding with me, I decided to call in at the British Embassy. This proved to be more diffcult than it sounds because it has moved from where the guidebook said it was supposed to be. My tour up and down the lift in the rather run-down block where His Excellency, Our Man in Havana, used to hang out was filmed for its humorous effect but there was, I suppose, a serious point to be made. Surely there should at least be a sign on the door to tell the distraught British visitor where his Embassy has transferred to?

By the time we found the new, temporary, Embassy building it was after-hours. We eventually established that the Ambassador was away and that no one really wanted to comment on Cuba from the British Government's point of view.

A queue of Cubans

The Cuban Government, however, wanted us to talk to the crowds queuing up outside the American Embassy, trying to get entry visas.

Actually, it is not the American Embassy. Since America and Cuba do not enjoy political relations, America is only represented in Havana by the American Special Interests section of the Swiss Embassy. But if it were an Embassy, it would be the biggest in Cuba.

You might think that the Cubans would be reluctant to show that dozens of people wait every day for an all-important interview in an attempt to get out of Cuba and into the hated America, but they do have a point to make.

America is no more generous in granting entry visas to Cubans than it is to any other nationality. However, if a Cuban sails to America in a home-made boat, he is automatically granted entry as a political refugee. A clear practical inducement to take to the water.

Anyway, we were supposed to do vox pops outside the Embassy with some people who were going to say it was not the Cubans who stopped people leaving Cuba but the Americans who stopped them getting into America. So we sought out people who had been kept waiting by American officials, or who had been refused entry, or required to come back month after month or even year after year to have their applications considered.

As it happens, though, we were waylaid by a political protest. An impassioned man, eyes bulging, screamed that it was absolute nonsense to say that the Americans were to blame. America was the only country in the world to take a stand on the human rights abuse in Cuba. It was not America's fault that so many Cubans wanted to leave their own country. He expected to be punished for speaking on-camera, but he no longer cared. He had been condemned to death thirty years before but not executed because he was too young at the time. He had received many death threats since then.

Louisa found all this too difficult to translate, but I got the gist. As did the rest of the crowd who, disgruntled with the United States, should have howled him down. Instead they all cheered him.

Street life

On another day I thought I had stumbled on evidence of genuine political discussion and exercise of free speech. In a square called Parc Centrale, a group of men appeared to be having an open-air meeting. Thirty or more of them were yelling and screaming. Now they were all one crowd, then they would divide into smaller groups. Were they political agitators? They were certainly very agitated. Perhaps it was the equivalent of Speaker's Corner? Here Louisa was able to help me. They were arguing about baseball. Baseball may be an all-American sport but it excites real Cuban emotion as well, and is played extensively throughout the island. These men were all beyond the age of actually playing. They had reached that age of man when he is only fit to argue the toss with the likes of Desmond Lynam and Jimmy Hill. So here they come every day, apparently, shouting each other down and putting the world of sport to rights. Lacking a working knowledge of both Spanish and baseball, I confined myself to advocating a change in the LBW law in Test cricket. Most of the crowd looked at me in astonishment, but several vociferously argued that the rules should be left well alone.

Eat, drink and be merry

We thought we had better investigate the unofficial side of life in Cuba. Being TV folk we naturally first thought of dinner. Regular restaurants in Havana are not particularly impressive, but we learnt that you can eat well enough on the black market.

I shall be discreet to protect my sources. Not far from one of the most touristy parts of Havana, Hasselbacher [not his real name] runs a restaurant in his house. You get to it through a front courtyard and it consists of a combined kitchen and dining room (and living room for Hasselbacher's family) leading on to another courtyard at the back, where they keep a pig. In the steaming kitchen Hasselbacher presides over his stoves, oblivious to boiling water and fat splashing on to his naked torso, while his wife and other relations sort out the plates and serve local take-away customers who come to the front courtyard.

The children wandered around the table legs and the family's puppy weed on the floor, but in these frankly squalid circumstances we ate the best meal of our stay in Cuba: a huge lobster served in a fantastic broth. (I cannot give you the recipe, Hasselbacher is protecting his sauces.)

All this is illegal for some reason – possibly because you have to pay in US dollars (I suppose the Health Inspectors could probably shut the restaurant down anyway) and Hasselbacher has even been to prison for his crime of providing what people want. He certainly would not let his restaurant appear on-camera, but if you go to Havana, I would recommend you find Hasselbacher's real name and address.

Since it was a family home, the family television was on in the corner. Cubans pick up American programmes using a variety of dustbin lids and tin foil dishes which would sadden the heart of any BSkyB salesman. But Cuba's own TV stations are pretty good as well. We were in Hasselbacher's a night or two after we had been to Mariel Harbour, and watched a live broadcast of Fidel Castro meeting the Pastors for Peace in a TV studio. Various Pastors we had met at the harbour were there being greeted by the Great Leader. So he was still alive.

Or was he? It may have been a trick of the light, or the effect of too much wine with the lobster, but the more I looked at him the more Castro looked like Frankie Howerd wearing a false beard. Now there's a conspiracy theory for you.

It was time to wend our way home, shrugging off the late-night shift of cigar salesmen, rum suppliers and girls anxious to show us the delights of Old Havana in their apartments.

There was another illicit night spot to visit. Yoya is a singer and hostess of her own salsa bar in central Havana. I was told that her bar was in some way illicit or unauthorized so I expected a sort of speakeasy with maybe a hatch to talk through. In fact the bar (again, really the front room of a house) opened directly on to the street so the sounds of its five-piece band (trumpets, guitar, drums) spilled out into the dark night. Clearly it was not regarded as a threat to the authorities.

Yoya herself was a large version of Eartha Kitt. As far as I know she only entertains in this little bar crammed with no more than thirty people, but she exuded star-quality, clasping me to her like an old friend, leading the singing and dancing and winking at the camera. There was no shortage of rum to drink but not quite enough glasses to drink it from. There was no talk of politics – the ostensible reason for our visit. Politics was not on anybody's mind. This was not Communist Cuba, or capitalist Cuba, but the Cuba of a good time and music.

The morning after

What could be better for the morning after than a religious experience?

On my first night in Havana I had been introduced to a Venezuelan called Hector. He was dressed all in white because he was being inducted into the Cuban religion known as *Santería*. This is a system of beliefs brought to Cuba by the African slaves. It recognizes a variety of spirits, gods and goddesses which over the centuries became identified with Christian saints, largely, it would seem, to avoid suppression by the Catholic authorities. It has an exotic voodoo quality to it and is increasingly popular in these troubled times. Even Fidel Castro himself is said to be a believer.

The day after my visit to Yoya's, Hector took me to the house of his mentor, Pupi Brinks. A *Santería* shrine was set up there. Up some rather crumbling outside stairs was another shrine to a related faith of Palo, or the Congo religion as Hector called it (the Congo is where this faith originated). This shrine was surrounded by offerings of foodstuffs and chicken and dolls' heads. Hector gave me a special, possibly holy, spirit to drink. There was not much room for the liquid in the bottle as it was crammed with a variety of chillies, peppers, herbs and spices, plus gunpowder. One spark and it would be holy smoke.

I did not have enough time to understand many of the tenets of this religion, but the music was easy enough to get into. Pupi instructs a collection of followers in the discipline of African-style drumming and the dancing which goes with it. So here was yet another crumbling, private house crammed full of sensuous excitement, this time in the morning as they were rehearsing for a performance. But rehearsing with gusto. Half-a-dozen drummers, bongo players and percussionists beat out powerful rhythms, while men, girls and boys danced enthusiastically to the beat. It was all quite intoxicating, although that might have been the spirit.

Leaving on a Lada

It was time to go on holiday. Varadero is a little peninsular or spit of land which sticks out into the Caribbean from the north coast of Cuba, about 80 miles east of Havana. It always was a holiday resort but in the new drive for tourist dollars it has been rapidly developed. I was driven there in a Lada taxi along the dual carriageway called the Via Blanca. There are not many other cars on the road. The whole thing looks like a fifties bypass serving thirties levels of traffic.

Along the first few miles there are fields of oil derricks or nodding donkeys with which the Cuban government is hoping to strike lucky. They already produce some oil but they would like to produce more. There is a smell of sulphur in the air – almost as strong as the smell in Havana when the power station smoke blows in the wrong direction – so perhaps there is some progress being made. Most of the nodding donkeys, though, seem to have forgotten how to nod and stand around rather forlornly in the fields.

Not far from a magnificent bridge I made the mistake of stopping at what looked like a motorway service station, a restaurant called the Moderno. I can only ask for beer, sandwiches and water in Spanish, but I might as well have been asking for *pâté de fois gras*. It was lunchtime but the café had nothing to eat or drink. It was open, and the staff were there, but there was nothing for them to serve. My mistake was in calling at a café for Cubans. Further along the road was a café with plenty to eat. That one is for foreigners.

Varadero is a holiday paradise with hotels and beaches which look exactly like hotels and beaches the world over. The sea here is crystal clear, the sky particularly blue and the sunshine fabulous. It is like every other holiday resort, except for the eerie absence of Americans. But there are plenty of other people – Canadians, Germans, even some Britons – lining up to come here. Eammon Donnelly, the Irish general manager of the Bella Costa Hotel, is very enthusiastic about the trading conditions in Cuba: strong central government, very well-educated and well-behaved staff. This was the positive side of the Cubans' complaints that they were producing the most literate head-waiters in the world and the brainiest whores.

Either way it illustrates the grim paradox. Only by having a well-developed socialist system do you produce staff with the education and attitude to serve in a capitalist palace.

And capitalist palace it is. Here the bloated tourist can eat until he bursts on an island where the bulk of the population is rationed to a few pounds of rice a month. The socialist revolution is being sustained by providing a playground for visitors from the free-enterprise world. The whole area of Varadero is notorious for the number of prostitutes who are attracted to the rich foreign visitors. But is Cuba prostituting itself and its revolution by getting its foreign income in this way?

I made my excuses and left, and went back to Havana to talk to the civil rights movement.

Going underground

Angela Herrera is the President of the Cuban Democratic Coalition, one of the many internal opposition groups in Cuba. When contacting her we tried to be as discreet as possible. We did not think we had any reason to fear for ourselves, but there are plenty of stories of people speaking to foreign media who are picked up once the media have left.

Hector (in the white baseball cap) bangs the drum for Santería, the religion brought to Cuba with the slave trade.

Angela Herrera is used to trouble from the authorities. According to Cuban American literature, her home is under continuous siege by the secret police. It was not as bad as that, but we assumed that her local CDR would notice a British TV team paying her a visit. To reduce our numbers we did without our official translator and, indeed, our film camera (we had the sort of video camera that any tourist might carry).

She lived in one of the apparently ubiquitous gloomy Havana flats. Angela has been arrested on countless occasions over the years and imprisoned, usually for short periods, but at one point had the prospect of a seven-year prison sentence hanging over her head. The previous year she had been on hunger strike. In court, Angela is not represented by lawyers – there would be no point.

Angela is very popular with Cuban American groups, especially because she is black. Cubans come in all shades of black and white and all points in-between, and as a national group they seem tolerably well integrated. But the vast majority of Cuban Americans lobbying in Washington are from the lighter end of the spectrum, which sustains the belief that it is only the rich and the white who object to Castro. He is said to remain most popular with blacks despite the fact that he is white and his chosen companions are more or less exclusively white as well.

Right from the word go, Angela objected to the revolution. 'Batista was nothing compared to Castro', and she is angry about the oppression she and her family suffer for claiming what she regards as the basic human right of self-expression. Identified as an 'opposition' family, they found life even harder than everyone else did. They were convinced that Angela's grandson was excluded from his school basketball team because of the family's political stance.

Angela was prepared to speak in public and has paid the penalty many times for having done so. How many others are too scared to speak their mind?

We filmed another scene on a video camera. Three young guys wanted to talk to us, on-camera, but they wanted their identities kept secret. None of them claimed to be political activists but they were all desperate to get away from Cuba. One had tried to escape in a little boat but had managed no more than 10 miles of the 90-mile journey. A baby had fallen overboard and the whole thing had been a dreadful farce. Another guy had made two attempts but had been arrested on both occasions and gone to gaol. The third said he would never dare try to escape. He had spent some time working in Czechoslovakia and was therefore a rich man in Cuba as he had been able to bring back a motor-bike and sell it.

Mr Azuguarry had assured me that Cubans were free to leave the country, but to these men that was a joke.

Did they blame the Americans for the poor economic conditions within Cuba? No, it was the system here in Cuba that was the problem. They had no future. All there was to do, said one in his broken English, was to 'drink rum, if you had the money, and fock'. He claimed that everybody hated Castro and wanted to leave, including all the members of his own family. (One of Castro's daughters made a highly publicized exit from the country. Castro's brother Raúl remains in power, as he has done for the last thirty-five years.)

Since these men were not in any way political activists their remarks seemed all the more poignant. The broken-English speaker was kind enough to say that it was a pleasure to talk to me because he was able to express himself freely for a short while. Normally he felt like a slave. I put it to him that the Government asserts there is free speech and democracy in Cuba. The suggestion was met with scorn.

Special interests

It was nearly time to leave Cuba. On our last day we finally got permission to interview an official in the American Special Interests section of the Swiss Embassy.

There is nothing very Swiss about the American Special Interests section. Opposite the building the Cubans have thoughtfully sited a billboard on which they can post one of their many anti-Yankee messages for the benefit of the Americans over the road. Inside, the offices are guarded by a detachment of Marines. A popular posting for marines?

Not really, as apparently there is a strict non-fraternization rule. A difficult rule to obey for a fit young Marine in a country where there are plenty of women keen on fraternizing, especially with anyone who has hard currency in his pocket.

Gene Bigler, the First Secretary, is tall, large and bearded. A great cuddly bear of a man who had been an academic before joining the Diplomatic Corps. Strangely, it had been almost as hard to get an interview with him as it had been to catch sight of Castro, but in the event he was as relaxed as all Americans seem to be on-camera.

I reminded Mr Bigler of the absurd efforts America had made to get rid of Castro over the previous thirty-five years. The CIA-backed Bay of Pigs Invasion mounted in 1961 by a collection of Cuban Americans had been an utter failure; the blowing up of an airliner had been murderous; the attempts to use thallium salts to make Castro's beard fall out, to poison him with a tuberculosis-impregnated diving suit, to send him exploding cigars, to kill him using *femmes fatales* and other nonsense had been utter farce.

Mr Bigler wryly agreed this must have provided some comic relief for students of international relations, but maintained that Cuba's human rights record justified America's opposition to Castro's government.

Wasn't it, I wondered, simply the longest sulk in history? American businesses had been nationalized and America could not stand this impudent left-wing upstart who was right on its doorstep. Why else would a blockade be maintained against Cuba, and yet China be granted most-favoured-nation status?

No, the United States was entitled to object to its citizens' capital being seized and to refuse to trade with a country whose policies it disapproved of, and anyway it was not a blockade, just an embargo.

Either way, does not America's refusal to trade with Cuba provide Castro with the perfect excuse for his country's woes?

Not at all. The ports of Mexico and South America were as close to Cuba as Miami. It was the Communist system which was at fault. The American embargo scarcely affects Cuba's comic well-being.

If that was so, one wonders why they bother imposing the embargo in the first place. Also such a theory ignores the overwhelming influence America has on world trade and the fact that under the Cuba Democracy Act (The Torricelli Bill) it is attempting to force foreign businesses and countries to break their links with Cuba as well.

I also put the point to him that, by allowing Cubans automatic political refugee status if they fetched up in American jurisdiction but no special deals in the issuing of visas, the US Government was inadvertently encouraging Cubans to risk their lives in little boats or even deliberately for the propaganda value.

No, that was the result of two separate policy considerations. In general, Mr Bigler addressed the issues expertly and diplomatically, but I wonder if behind it all there is considerable embarrassment at the position America finds itself in with relation to Cuba. For all its influence in the world, America is trapped on this issue. The sanctions America uses against Cuba, whether you call them a blockade or an embargo, look like a sledge-hammer to crack a nut. And the fact of the matter is that the nut is still there. China is too big to shut out, but Cuba is too close for comfort.

While Castro remains in power, America looks impotent, but if Cuba's economy collapses altogether, will Communism or America get the blame?

One important factor in maintaining America's total opposition to Castro and all his works is that the million or more Cuban Americans are an extremely powerful and vocal political force. So my next step was to go back to Miami to meet some of them.

I have already mentioned Jorge Mas Conosa, the grandfather or perhaps godfather of the Cuban American Community. He agreed to see me in his office in the middle of the day on which his company was completing a take-over of some size. Mr Mas Conosa is not a large man but he is very powerful. He delivers lectures rather than answers questions and must be a formidable force in Washington where he argues the Cuban American's case from a right-wing perspective. He has been an exile for a long time. An opponent of Batista, he was an exile even before Castro came to power. He is fiercely anti-Communist and anti-Castro.

Castro, he insisted, has turned Cuba from one of the richest Latin American countries to one of the poorest. He will not have it that Cuba under Castro has achieved anything remarkable in the social or medical sphere. Costa Rica has done just as well and, in any case, was an improvement in medical care worth the arrests and imprisonment and exiles? More than one-fifth of Cubans now live in exile.

He did not think it anomalous that America imposed trade sanctions on Cuba. He rattled off a list of other countries to which these restrictions had applied. And why, he asked, was it all right for England to have imposed sanctions on South Africa because of its human rights record, but not all right to do the same to Cuba?

Like many Cuban Americans, he has become very successful in America but is keen to go back to rebuild Cuba. Strangely, if he ever gets his chance, he would probably rebuild it in America's likeness, so the long-term effect of Castro's revolution may be to make Cuba even more Americanized than it was when he took over.

A more impressive anti-Castro witness was the security guard just coming on duty in the office block as I was leaving. He told me he had been a political prisoner in Cuba, where he had been closely confined in a cell with other prisoners. They all had to urinate and defecate where they stood. He and his fellow prisoners were fed practically nothing. If their wives or girlfriends brought food when they visited them at the prison they would be subjected to intimate and offensive searches. He had eventually been released in the Mariel boat-lift, when Castro emptied his prisons and allowed America to take a motley collection of political prisoners like himself, plus pimps, drug-runners and mental patients. More than 100 000 people in all. But, he said rather quietly, even here in

Brothers to the rescue. Carlos nervously contemplates taking to the air with an inexperienced co-pilot.

America where he has found freedom, people do not really want to listen when you tell them of experiences like that. They do not believe you.

I want to be in America

The next day I flew with *Hermanos Al Rescate,* or Brothers to the Rescue. This is a group of volunteer Cuban Americans who fly little four-seater planes from the coast of Florida out over the sea to spot people fleeing Cuba in their home-made boats. The US Coastguard does not have the resources to maintain sufficient patrols but does respond when it is informed of sinking boats or people washed up on a rocky island. (Brothers to the Rescue do not do any of the picking-up themselves.)

There is some danger in this activity. On the day I flew with them, a senior member of the group was suffering from a broken leg which he had sustained in a recent accident, and another young man was getting used to a wheelchair, having been paralysed from the waist down from another crash. As he checked our plane, Carlos, my pilot, wished to assure me that these were both incidents caused by mechanical failure rather than pilot error.

Brothers to the Rescue fly over the ocean looking for a raft. This can be as pathetic as a few planks of wood tied together, or even only a couple of tractor tyres. Some rafts have outboard motors, some just drift with the current. Some make it, some do not. Some get picked up by Cuban gunboats before they reach Florida. Some sink.

Only 90 miles separate Cuba from Miami, but that is oceans of ocean to get lost in. But if these people make it, they have really made it.

As we flew on, looking for a raft of people to whom we could throw a message and a marker flare, it struck me that this was a satisfying activity for these volunteers. Not as self-indulgent as merely island-hopping would be, not as dangerous as going off to war. Self-sacrifice and good fun in one package. It was hard not to get carried along by their enthusiasm, and equally hard not to have a good time flying around in the sky.

In the aircraft hangar there is a woman called Maggie who organizes things back at base while the aircraft are in the air. She can remember, as a young girl, being really excited by Castro's revolution. She reckoned that Castro had the support of 90 per cent of the Cuban population, but within a year everything had gone sour. She was glad to get away, as were the people spotted in the sea that day.

For years I can remember Cuba being held up as an example of what Communism can achieve, and Castro was heralded as a leader who remained popular with his people. Opponents of Communism explained this away as being the result of the subsidies and help that Cuba received from the Soviet Union. Now the boot is on the other foot. And it is Castro's failures which now have to be explained away, usually by referring to the American blockade or boycott. The only thing worse than trading with the enemy is not trading with the enemy.

The sad thing about the Cuban revolution is that, even in its own terms, it has failed. The buildings are falling down, the people are desperately poor, desperate to get away or simply desperate. Political prisoners are in the gaols, prostitutes are on the streets, the American dollar is in demand: the very conditions that inspired the revolution in the first place. But perhaps it is true that all revolutions eventually bring things full-circle.

I had an hour or two left to walk along the smart streets of Miami Beach. As I strolled past its shops crammed with stylish clothes, its restaurants and fast-food stores and bars offering every sort of delight, it struck me what a paradise in material terms this must seem to a half-starved Cuban refugee who washes up here after several days at sea and several years on subsistence-level rationing. In 500 yards, though, I was approached by four beggars asking me if I could spare any change.

At least I wasn't mugged.

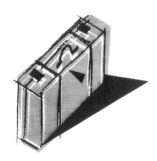

Our Man In...

DOMINICA

DOMINICA

Portsmouth

Melville Hall
Airport

Carib Reserve

Trafalgar Falls

Roseau

Scotts Head

0   Miles   10
0   Kilometers   50

Florida

Bahamas

Cuba

Haiti

Jamaica

Puerto   Virgin   Anguilla &
Rico   Islands   St Martin

Barbuda
Antigua

Dominican
Republic

St Kitts & Nevis

Guadeloupe

Dominica

Honduras

Caribbean Sea

Martinique
St Lucia

Barbados

Windward Islands

Nicaragua

St Vincent & The Grenadines

Grenada

Columbia

Venezuela

LEAVE TO ENTER
FOR
EMPLOYMENT PROHIBITED
COMMONWEALTH OF DOMINICA
MELVILLE HALL AIRPORT

AS island paradises go, Dominica is not well-known. Its name does not help. Christopher Columbus spotted the island on 3 November 1493, which happened to be a Sunday, and it has been called after the Latin word for the Sabbath more or less ever since.

Explorers were always doing that sort of thing – Easter Island, Man Friday, Sheffield Wednesday – but it is not always useful. Certainly with Dominica, the name does not really capture the essence of the place. It implies a special connection with the Lord's Day or Latin America, when in reality it has neither. It is actually a former British colony, with an English-speaking population retaining strong links with the Commonwealth and the United Kingdom.

But mispronounce Dominica, as many people do, and it is easy to confuse it with its much larger Caribbean neighbour, the Spanish-speaking Dominican Republic (Haiti's other half in the island of Hispaniola). Worse than that, pronounce it correctly, as Domi-*nee*-ca, and it is easy to confuse it with the greatest hit record of the Singing Nun.

It is not much better writing it down. A good deal of mail intended for Dominica gets misdirected to the Dominican Republic, even if you use its correct title, 'The Commonwealth of Dominica'.

Quite apart from the problems of its own name, Dominica is an island in a sea of confusing nomenclature. The Caribbean Islands, especially those once owned by Britain, are often referred to as the West Indies. (Another of Columbus's contributions; he thought he had got to India when actually he had sailed West across the Atlantic. St Columbus is the patron saint of baggage handlers.)

The term 'West Indies' lives on chiefly as the name of the cricket team assembled from players who come from a variety of now quite separate independent countries brought together to humiliate the all-England team of Robin Smith, Allan Lamb and Graeme Hick. Plus Philip De Freitas, who was in fact born in Dominica.

Dominica forms part of a chain of islands called the Antilles, or more specifically the Lesser Antilles, as any atlas will tell you. In my experience you seldom come across the term 'Lesser Antilles' or 'Greater Antilles' in everyday life. Within the Lesser Antilles, Dominica is part of the Windward Islands. Dominican bananas are normally sold as Windward Island Bananas, although, as it happens, until the Second World War Dominica was regarded as one of the Leeward Islands. Perhaps the wind of change was blowing around the area at the time.

The complication of all these geographical terms is matched by the untidy colonial history of the region. Looking down the Antilles in an atlas, one finds islands with allegiances, or former allegiances, to Britain,

France, Spain, Holland and the United States of America. It is an apparently random pattern of political and linguistic attachments produced by the ebb and flow of military and maritime fortunes two or three hundred years ago. The epitome of this illogicality must be the tiny island of St Martin (also known as Sint Maarten) which, despite having an area of less than 25 square miles, is divided in jurisdiction between Holland and France. Why they don't just give it to Belgium and have done with it, goodness only knows.

Dominica is not quite as complicated as that. It was fought over by the French and the British right up to the beginning of the nineteenth century. Britain ultimately prevailed, but there is a local French-based patois and quite a number of French words which have found their way into everyday (English) speech.

In fact, Dominica is now located between what are officially two French departments, Martinique and Guadeloupe. The French notion of decolonization is to alter the status of a colony to a county, and then insist that no one notices that these departments are to be found thousands of miles from the mainland.

Dominica was one of the last of the Caribbean islands to be conquered, colonized or otherwise taken from the Carib people by the European powers after the New World was 'discovered'. Approaching Dominica, especially by air, one can immediately see why. It is almost entirely made of densely wooded, steeply sloped mountains and valleys. There are practically no beaches to provide easy landing points. Altogether very difficult territory to invade. No doubt as a result of that, there is an area of Dominica in which the last survivors of the Carib people are still living. To have a reservation on one island in a sea named after them may not be much, but I suppose it is something.

Dominica is a challenging place to invade, and also a challenging place to make an economic success. Its lack of beaches limits its attraction to tourists, so it has avoided the destructive force of tourism. But it also misses out on the income now enjoyed by St Lucia, and almost all of the nearby islands, which comes from holiday-makers heading for a paradise which has to include a white sand beach where you can lie in the sun before or after or instead of swimming in the sea.

At different times in its history, Dominica has enjoyed some fairly prosperous periods growing sugar, limes or vanilla, but for the past forty years it has made its living from bananas. This banana trade is, however, under threat. Bananas grown here are produced by independent farmers on remote mountain small-holdings. Bigger, fatter and cheaper bananas are produced on bigger, flatter and more profitable plantations in Costa

Rica and other Latin American countries. How serious is the threat to Dominica's banana trade, and how serious would it be for Dominica if the trade were to collapse altogether?

Finding out was the reason for my visit.

Just off the banana boat

The trade in bananas with Dominica, and all the Windward Islands, is conducted by one company: Geest.

A leisurely way to arrive in the Windward Islands is to get there by a Geest banana boat. Setting off from Southampton, it takes eight days to cross the Atlantic, eight days to go from island to island, and eight days to sail home again.

There is room for twelve passengers. And they make the crossing in style: black tie for dinner, gin slings and Scrabble for recreation. Plus food of the highest order. It is all redolent of an age when there was more pink on the map than on Barbara Cartland's cocktail dress. There are dozens

One of Geest's fleet. You have to be rich or bananas to cross the Atlantic in this.

of cruise ships which ply their trade up and down the Caribbean, but this one is different. A banana boat is not like a cruise ship (cruise ships are really far too Billy Butlin, according to virtually all twelve of Geest's passengers) and has the disadvantage of not being as stable in rough weather. I joined the Geest boat to get to Dominica, but only after it had reached the Caribbean and had already weathered several storms in the Atlantic. It had been a particularly rough crossing, but by the time I joined the passengers they had recovered their composure and were, on the face of it, having a very good time indeed.

They were certainly all in a healthy frame of mind to tuck into a five-course dinner which featured some excellent crab backs (a local delicacy), and Beef Wellington, a suitably imperial reminder of home. They took in their stride the intrusion of me and my film crew, and I was berated on all sides one for being so easy to confuse with Clive James – same name, same lack of hair, eyes and neck. I am pretty sure they could have kept up joshing of this sort for the entire twenty-four days if I had been with them for the whole voyage.

A banana boat is not a cheap way to travel and not everyone would enjoy being tossed around for nearly a month in the company of eleven other well-heeled fellow travellers. Your travel plans do sometimes have to be changed at short notice to accommodate the demands of the bananas, but Geest have no difficulty in filling their very well-appointed cabins.

It is all very old-fashioned, quirky and British. And like everything else which is old-fashioned, quirky and British, it is not going to last.

To me the ways of business are strange: Geest make a profit on their passengers, which must, you would think, be a comfort when the income from bananas can go down as well as up, and sometimes threatens to disappear altogether. However, as and when they replace their banana boats, the people at Geest who decide these things are getting rid of the passenger accommodation. Apparently it costs a lot to fit out a ship with cabins and so forth, and takes eight years to recoup that money from the fares. And that is not fast enough. Compared with the time it will take to make money on the Channel Tunnel, or most skyscrapers in London, eight years must be a drop in the ocean, but there you have it. Next week a big-businessman will explain why it made sense to keep London's Centre Point empty for twenty years.

Anyway, bidding a fond farewell to Captain Flannagan, and the passengers with whom he dines every night, I jumped ship in Dominica. In the meantime, bananas were getting on board. They were being brought from all over the island, checked, weighed, graded and loaded.

Boxes are put on to pallets and pallets are put on to the ship using cranes. Occasionally there is a crash, and some bananas setting out on the long journey to an English fruit bowl fall at the first hurdle. The dock-workers, like dockers and packers the world over, bear these occasional accidents with equanimity, and are allowed to take a few damaged bananas home with them.

Banana splits

Dominica has been an independent nation since 1978. Its trading arrangements as far as bananas are concerned go back to colonial times, and its critics say they still smack of the days of the Empire.

In the thirties, bananas which grew well in the Caribbean (they need lots of sunshine and rain) were chosen as a crop to bring cash to the Windward Islands and fruit to Britain. The Second World War rather disrupted things but afterwards the trade resumed and in 1954 Geest took over the shipping of bananas, and things really began to prosper.

Geest was a successful British horticultural firm, founded by two Dutch brothers, whose original business was importing bulbs from Holland. Its move into importing bananas from the Windward Islands was a spectacular success. Geest came to outstrip Fyffes and Jamaica Producers (both of whom import bananas from Jamaica) as banana suppliers to Britain. Geest currently imports about 60 per cent of the UK's bananas.

Under more or less paternalistic arrangements, the Windward Islands were allowed a protected market. The Windwards and Geest have prof-ited from the deal. And the contract with Geest was renewed after Dominica's independence. Under this contract, Geest buy all the bananas from Dominica's producers and ship them to Britain. (The same arrange-ment applies on the other Windward islands.) Geest gets the best price it can from the retailers in the UK and pays the farmers, but only after it has deducted the cost of shipping, ripening and marketing the bananas, and taken its own profit on all those operations. The ordinary farmer has to bear his own costs, such as paying for fertilizer and vehicles. The farmer might receive about 10 per cent of the retail price of the banana.

It is anything but a free market. Dominica's farmers and Geest's profits rely upon the preferential tariff protection of the British govern-ment. There is much to recommend the arrangement. It is difficult for a small island like Dominica to produce anything in large enough quan-tities to make it economical to transport it to the rest of the world. Having one product and a guaranteed market solves many of these

problems. But there are obvious dangers. Being dependent on one crop, dependent on one company, dependent on one foreign government's preferential tariff protection makes the Dominicans, well over-dependent.

Disease, or a hurricane, might ruin the banana crop, but as it is the dangers on the horizon are the Single European Market and the GATT Trade Deal. There is not a great deal that Dominicans can do about either of these things, but they are increasingly doubting whether it is a great deal that they get from Geest.

Mind you, Shelford Scotland, the first man I talked to on the island, was not minded to criticize the arrangements. He thought the forty-year old contract with Geest was an excellent one. Up and down the island he sees people able to afford 4-wheel drive pick-ups and cars, there is food in the shops and wealthy-looking people. All right, it is forty years with one company. But if you are with a wife for forty years, and you're happy with her, why change her?

ABOVE AND RIGHT: *Loading loads of bananas.*

Well, Scottie, as he is known, has worked for Geest for most of the forty years they have been trading. He is now the manager of their dock-side operations in Dominica. So I suppose he would say that, but I went off to explore the island and to see if his view was in the majority.

The main town of Dominica is Roseau. It is a sleepy little place made up for the most part of streets of little wooden buildings with brightly painted balconies. It has a dour Roman Catholic cathedral and a large Anglican church. There are some other public buildings but mostly it is small-scale and low-key. It has a waterfront promenade which looks very familiar, as well it might, having been built recently by McAlpine. It is one corner of a foreign field which is forever Frinton. Nearby is an unusual plaque which says:

The British were here, thank God.

I say it is unusual. Perhaps there is one like it in Dublin.

As a rule I am not one for feeling guilt about the actions of my countrymen before I was born. Nor, to be fair, would I claim any credit for their success. But there is something dreadful about realizing that almost the entire population of an island like Dominica is there only because their ancestors were slaves brought on British and other European ships. It is particularly dreadful because, even by the standards of the day, I would suggest it was an entirely immoral thing to do. Certainly slavery was not recognized or lawful within England itself, as a slave-owner discovered to his cost in 1772. He brought his slave home from the West Indies, whereupon the slave, James Sommersett, brought an action for *habeas corpus*. The judge, Lord Mansfield, found in the slave's favour, ending his judgment with the resounding cry, 'The Black must be discharged.' (Sommersett's Case, 20 St. Tr. 1.)

Nowadays, Roseau looks a simple sort of place, not rich but not stricken with poverty. Undeveloped rather than underdeveloped. And quiet. Except that when I arrived it was carnival time.

Carnival celebrates the beginning of Lent or the end of slavery or something like that. You get carnivals all over the Caribbean and in Dominica you get them all over the island. On Monday and Shrove Tuesday there are two days of dancing in the streets, drinking to excess, music to burst the eardrums, costumes, displays and parades. In England, we make pancakes.

Actually, it is obvious that the British influence is still strong as the whole thing is clearly modelled on the Notting Hill Carnival.

Mostly, the carnival consists of a procession of large lorries carrying even larger sound systems. There are a few live bands but recorded music predominates. Either way the music is loud enough to make your heart cavity vibrate to the bass beat. Presumably the flimsy wooden buildings can only survive this annual onslaught because they are built to withstand hurricane-force winds.

During the day, groups of youngsters and oldsters dress up in co-ordinated costumes: as angels, Egyptians, local firemen or London policemen; but as the day wears on it is the individuals with their individual idea of what to wear who catch the eye. One guy washes himself from time to time, covering his body in soap suds at key points on the procession route, others wear Wellington boots and swimming trunks. It is as though the whole island has suddenly dived into a dressing-up box. A large number of men dress in women's clothes. They do not seem to be camping it up, or even playing for laughs like pantomime dames. Nobody could explain to me why this is so popular. Maybe they are related to Tory MPs.

Most of the time the sun shines on what is undoubtedly a carnival atmosphere, but every now and then there is a rain shower which lasts for a few minutes. However, this is ignored by the crowd and it just goes away.

As the evening wears on, the crowds in the narrow streets develop a sort of rhythmic shuffle. Not so much a dance as a very energetic bus queue. Young and old people join in, the really energetic having started at 4 a.m. on the Monday with the opening event (this is called *Jové* and is when things are really wild).

The jump-up continues that afternoon and evening and all day Tuesday. The action ends at 8 p.m. by order of the police. This is to prevent the wild behaviour and violence which apparently happened on previous years. The ordinance is not popular but is obeyed with more or less a good grace.

The population of Dominica is about 70 000. That is less than it takes to fill Wembley Stadium. But while the carnival is on, it is as noisy as Wembley with a Cup Final taking place plus three or four rock concerts happening at the same time.

The music is highly repetitive with two or three high-volume calypsos coming round and round again. One, called *Kool Pipe,* has a message about Aids and safe sex. (There is a dangerously erotic feel to carnival music.) More popular is *Tiwé Yo.* The words are local patois for 'take them out'. This means throw away the rotten fruit and, by extension, kick out those responsible for the running of the banana trade. Ultimately this means get rid of the ruling Dominica Freedom Party and its leader Prime Minister, Dame Eugenia Charles.

LEFT: *Roseau in regular mood.* ABOVE: *Dame Eugenia Charles at home.*
TOP: *Roseau in carnival atmosphere.*

ABOVE: *Clement Ferreira listens patiently to my recreation of a classic Sooty and Sweep episode while* (LEFT) *one of the workers on his estate tends to some young bananas.*

be applied and they soon run off the steep slopes. But the banana is, taken as a whole, always willing.

Many of the bunches around the island are grown inside blue plastic bags. It looks as though they produce their own wrapping ready for Sainsburys' shelves. In fact the bags are put on to accelerate growth, in the same way that an English cold frame works. Clement does not trouble to do this, reckoning the labour cost of putting on the bags outweighs the economic gain of faster growing times.

Botanically, the banana plant is a monocotyledon, a term which describes how many leaves it produces when its seed germinates. This puts it in the same category as grass. Banana trees grow to a height of 10 feet or more, but basically they are just overgrown bits of lawn. Although that is rather like dismissing a tiger as a jumped-up tabby cat, or a Great Dane as nothing more than a dachshund with high suspension.

As arranged on Dominica, banana plantations are agreeable and relaxing. Work is quite labour-intensive, with banana hands having to hack back leaves and branches with machetes and in due course pick the grown fruit. But for a great deal of the time the banana trees just lap up the sun and the rain showers and produce bananas by the handful.

Clement Ferreira cannot see himself staying in bananas much longer, however much he likes them. The banana is willing, but the price is weak. At the price they are fetching at the moment, he is not making a profit at all. But he has no alternative way to make a living. Dame Eugenia had outlined a number of schemes to improve things including one to organize the workers into entrepreneurial units, travelling round the farms hiring out their labour and using their own pick-up trucks. She seemed to pin some hopes on this to raise the living standards of the workers while lowering labour costs to the farmers. But Clement dismissed this notion out of hand. He would still have to run his own pick-up truck to travel round the island and get his bananas to the ship. Why would he want to pay for the use of someone else's pick-up as well?

No, he would be out of bananas by next April, if things did not improve. I wonder for how many years he has been saying that. And whether this year it may turn out to be true.

Cletina Benjamin has got out of bananas. She started in bananas by carrying boxes of them at the dockside, supporting herself when she was fifteen and pregnant with her first child. She progressed over the years to the position where she was able to buy 4 acres of banana plantation when Geest were selling off the land they owned on Dominica (they no longer own any here). She explains she had to sell one of her acres to a housing development to pay for the land she had bought. In fact, she got as much for that single acre as she had paid for the whole lot, which sounds like a good deal, but it just was not practicable for her to support herself on her remaining 3 acres. And as she explained as she sat outside her small wooden house, Geest no longer pick up bananas from Portsmouth (her local town), so she would have to transport them to Roseau. This is more expensive both in fuel and in the almost inevitable damage to the easily bruised bananas as they bounce around in the back of a pick-up.

Cletina can still eat her own bananas and sell some coconuts from her few coconut trees, but she does not farm the bananas as such. In fact I could not quite grasp how she makes a living. Her daughter, Anne Marie, is not interested in bananas at all. She appears to spend all her time at the moment travelling to and from Barbados in an attempt to get a visa to study in America.

In a particularly remote part of the island we tracked down Vanoulst John Charles. Everybody knows Vanoulst, which is just as well as his banana farm is high up in the hills where the long and winding roads have given way to tracks and ordinary vehicles have given way to Land Rovers. Signposts are not a strong point anywhere on the island; up in the hills they are non-existent. But everyone we spoke to on the way knew where we could find Vanoulst, even though we had to be given directions five or six times before we were able to track him down.

He is a self- (and rather well-) educated man. Tall and thin and in his sixties, he has been in bananas and Dominican politics all his life. He was a founder member of Dame Eugenia's Dominican Freedom Party, but later fell out with her and her party's policies. He had served as the President of Winban, the quango set up to represent the Windward Island banana industry. He maintained that the various Prime Ministers of the various Windward Islands had not been firm enough with Geest over the years. Dame Eugenia (and others), for all her iron lady image, had not got rid of the old colonial attitudes which still paid too much respect to people and institutions from overseas.

Vanoulst resented the profit that Geest made from his bananas. The Windwards did not need Geest: they should have their own ships, do their own marketing and so on. I pointed out that farmers always resent money being made out of their crop by those who package it, transport it, retail it. An English farmer does not normally own the lorries which take his crop from the countryside to the city, nor does he make any money from its retail and distribution. Why should Dominican farmers be any different? And with banana prices low and getting lower, was this really the time for these islands to start investing in banana boats and ripening sheds in England, risking even more money in the process?

Bananas are the only fruit.

He dismissed all those arguments with a grin. This should have been done years ago. The Third World just gets worse and worse off. The price of bananas and all other agricultural commodities goes up, or more usually down, because of economic conditions in the First World. The price of vehicles and chemicals such as fertilizers goes down, or more usually up, because of economic conditions in the First World. The Third World does not get a look-in. It is then granted aid representing only a fraction of the cost that these changes have imposed. And what is more, the Third World countries do not co-operate with each other, but compete. The good price of Dominican bananas was being undercut by Latin American banana growers whose workers were paid a pittance. So if they take all the banana trade, the Third World, will, overall, have grown even poorer.

This rather depressing analysis was said in a charming and good-natured way. Vanoulst is never without a twinkle in his eye. He seemed certain that Geest had done too well out of the Windward Islands and that the farmers had been ripped off. His whole livelihood is under threat, but he is content to discuss the problem with less rancour than a couple of cricket fans analysing a Test Match defeat.

Vanoulst's large estate is high up in the hills. His trees are therefore particularly exposed to wind damage but their lofty position does make his corner of paradise particularly beautiful. Stretching to the horizon is a Jurassic Parkland of jagged mountain peaks and emerald forests decorated with puffs of white clouds and swirling mists.

As we spoke, a few of Vanoulst's workers sheltered from the gentle rain in one of the many shacks dotted around the countryside while they packed bananas in their boxes ready to be driven off and put on the next boat to England. Playing at Vanoulst's feet was a pretty two-year-old girl – his latest and thirteenth child. The child's mother, an equally pretty twenty-year-old, helped with the packing. It just shows what bananas can do for you.

Yes, but what if we have no bananas?

Early next day I flew to St Lucia to see Willie Rapier, Geest's head man in the Windward Islands. Geest's headquarters in the Windwards are now in Castries, which is St Lucia's main town.

Island-hopping in a small plane in the Caribbean must be one of the most joyous activities possible. I dare say nautical types would insist that it is better by boat. And railway buffs would resent not having some solid track beneath their feet. But to fly like a bird, oh me, oh my …

As you skirt round Dominica, you can understand why it has no beaches. The steep line of the hills appears to keep going straight down to the water's edge. Here and there you spot a few fringes of sand but nothing much to write, or to send a postcard, home about.

The sea is overpoweringly blue. Alongside the various greens of the hills, the whole place looks like a new paintbox before a child has got to it and messed it up to produce the muddier tones we are used to in Britain.

The one-hour flight takes us over Martinique. Of course I am cheating because I know it is French, but Martinique definitely *looks* French from the air. You cannot actually see the croissants in the cafés but you know they are there. It has large, flat, open fields like you get for miles and miles around Paris. It does not have the mountains of Dominica, and if it once had a rainforest it is long gone. The island is more built-up, developed I suppose is the word, and much, much drier.

We do not have a chance to see a great deal of St Lucia from the air, but its landscape is approximately a cross between Dominica and Martinique. It does have inviting white sand beaches and is pretty well built-up. But there are also green hills and forests towards the centre of the island.

I had been to St Lucia a few years before, and it seemed to me that Castries had doubled in size in less than ten years. Having said that, on my previous visit I had not sought out Geest's headquarters in an unprepossessing office building in an industrial corner of the town, so I may be getting a different impression this time round.

Willie Rapier is tall and stoops down to talk to ordinary-sized mortals. His shape, plus a slightly yellowy skin, invites the thought that he is growing, just slightly, to look like the fruit he has been trading in all his working life. He speaks with a soft, slightly West Indian accent. He points out that the contract with Geest has been in existence for forty years and it is only now, when times are hard, that people are claiming that the contract is no good.

It is true that Geest have a monopoly under the deal, but the deal is to take *all* the bananas that the farmers produce. Not such a bad deal. If two or three competitors called each week or month, none of them would be able to give this guarantee. Geest have been very successful in building up their ripening sheds in Britain, as well as good trading contacts throughout the country to ensure a market for the Windward Islanders' crop. Perhaps Geest cannot expect to be thanked, but it is a bit much to be criticized for having done their part of the job well over the years.

Yes, yes, but are Geest going to abandon Dominica now? Willie says Geest will always take bananas if Dominica is producing them.

This expert phrase is, I suppose, intended to be an assurance, but it means very little. If the Dominicans cannot make money out of bananas, they will stop growing them, and that in itself would leave Geest free to go elsewhere. Indeed they are already going somewhere else, having acquired banana plantations in Central America.

This, Willie Rapier maintains, is just by way of increasing volume, so that Geest's overall strength is improved. They are not preparing a bolt hole in case the Windward Islands trade goes belly-up. They are not, of course, mutually exclusive.

Throughout our conversation, Willie Rapier was charm personified. But a worrying picture is emerging. Geest own no estates on Dominica, although they do in Latin America. They are not building any more boats to cruise passengers around this pattern of islands. They do not have to trade in Dominican bananas; the Dominicans do.

The fact is that Geest are in business to make money, and for forty years they have done just that. No doubt they would be happy to continue to do that in the Windward Islands for another forty years, but only if conditions remain favourable.

And what are the alternatives to dealing with Geest?

Geest are a big company in the Windward Islands and in Britain, but in the world – even in the world of bananas – they are tiny. They ship only 1.6 per cent of world banana exports. Most of the world banana trade is controlled by the three American companies: United Brands, Standard Fruit and Del Monte. And nobody claims any of those would treat the Windward Islands more generously than Geest. These companies' records over many years make Geest look benign in the extreme.

At Dominica's most renowned beauty spot, the Trafalgar Falls, I chatted to Atherton Martin. As an ecologist, he reckons that a monocrop is always doomed to failure, whether from disease, disaster or disruption of some sort. Diversification is the answer.

But would it be worth the while of Geest, or anyone else, sending a refrigerated banana boat to pick up only a fraction of the bananas produced today? Could anything other than concentration on bananas have provided the steadily growing prosperity that the island has enjoyed since the war? Could small amounts of citrus fruits compete on the open market?

There is an established coconut products industry. And there is certainly room for the Caribbean islands to supply each other's wants, rather than each of them seeking markets in America and Europe to earn

ABOVE: *High up in the hills in the north of the island I found farmer Vanoulst John Charles to be provocative, entertaining and enthusiastic despite his complaints about the treatment of the Third World.*
RIGHT: *The Trafalgar Falls. I bet none of the Francophone islands have anything as wonderful as this.*

money to import basic requirements back home again. Because of its underdeveloped tourist industry, Dominica does not have an international airport. By that, I mean one to which you can fly direct in a jumbo jet. Atherton makes the point that it is quite unnecessary for every island to have its own full size runway. No community of 70 000 people in Europe would expect such a thing. To take a random example, the London Borough of Islington has a population twice that size but is content to share the few airports in and around London with the other thirty-two London boroughs and the rest of the South East of England.

Atherton Martin was at least optimistic. Unusual in an ecologist, in my experience. Dominica has a good water supply and a cheap hydro-electric power supply. It has not been spoiled by tourism in the past and so, oddly enough, can look forward to a future in nature tourism for people who come to walk or swim in the natural world without doing as much damage to the environment as a package tourist.

A lady called Grace Tung had an even more outlandish way for Dominica to make money. She is Chinese and has introduced a scheme whereby Taiwanese or people from Hong Kong can invest a minimum of US$35 000 in the island and acquire Dominican citizenship. This sounds like selling your birthright, but over dinner in a Chinese restaurant in Roseau – in fact, the only Chinese restaurant in Roseau – Grace Tung explained it was not that, nor even selling passports. Other countries, even Canada, went in for something along those lines, but this scheme involved investing in a particular project, and then getting a passport. It was not like selling a passport at all. It all sounded a bit desperate, though I understand that residents of Hong Kong find it easier to get into Britain if they arrive with a pile of money, so it may be that nobody is in a position to criticize.

Queen for an hour

By happy chance the Queen chose to visit Dominica just as I was leaving. In fact she was only going to touch down at Melville Hall Airport in order to refuel. She was on her way, with the Duke of Edinburgh, from Anguilla to Guyana on a Caribbean tour. With no sign of a Dimbleby in sight I attempted a commentary for our film, but it was all very low-key. Very British, in fact, even down to the shower of rain which threatened to, but did not quite ruin, the whole thing. I was able to point out that the Queen was wearing a blue outfit (she even had a matching blue sling to support an arm injured in a riding accident), and the Duke of Edinburgh was in grey.

She met Prime Minister Dame Eugenia Charles, plus Dominica's President, as well as Commissioner Blanchard and several other dignitaries. There was just enough time for tea and sandwiches and a full tank of aviation spirit, and she was off again. I think it was Billy Connolly who noted that the Queen must think that Britain smells of fresh paint. She certainly must imagine that the entire Commonwealth is populated by politicians, policemen in white gloves and school children whose main hobby is waving little Union Jacks. She did not notice me among the cheering children, but I am almost sure that Baroness Chalker, who was with the royal party, nodded briefly at me as she went past.

Anyway, it was time for me to leave too. Since I had found everybody so charming on this pretty island I rather hoped they could hang on to their banana trade. I arrived home in England determined to eat only Dominican bananas as far as possible. A protected market in bananas seems the Dominicans' only hope, unless and until Atherton Martin's notion of a diversified economic base takes root.

In my local supermarket in London I was still reflecting on how difficult it must be to export foodstuffs, or any other products, from remote islands given the transport costs and so on. But I was pleased to find Windward Islands bananas on sale and, for the moment, still going strong. And onions grown in Tasmania.

Our Man In...

MAASAI MARA

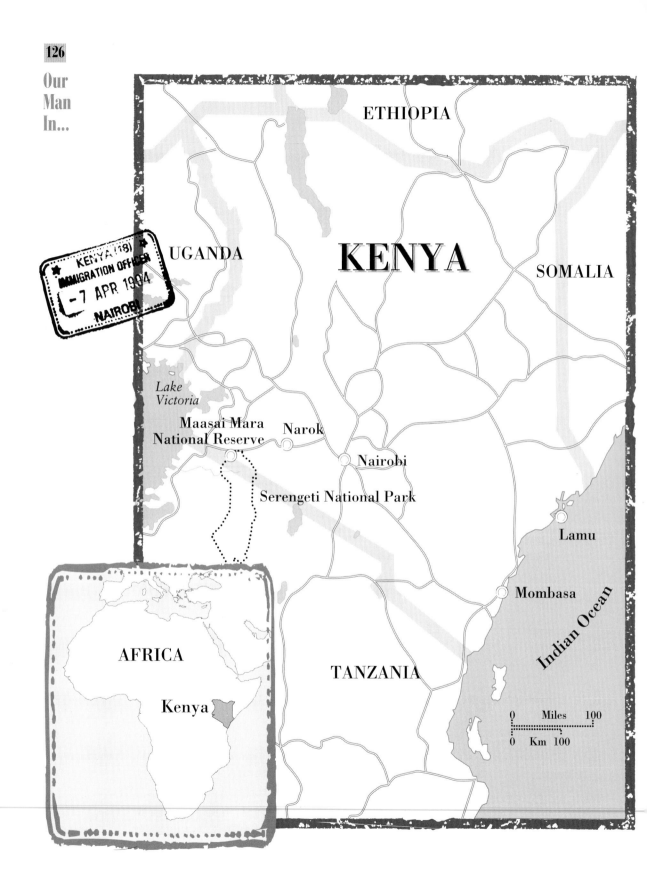

ETHIOPIA

UGANDA

KENYA

SOMALIA

Lake
Victoria

Maasai Mara
National Reserve

Narok

Nairobi

Serengeti National Park

Lamu

Mombasa

Indian Ocean

AFRICA

Kenya

TANZANIA

0   Miles   100

0   Km   100

KENYA (18)
IMMIGRATION OFFICER
-7 APR 1994
NAIROBI

KENYA has been a favourite of mine since I spent a few months there between school and university more than twenty years ago. A careless remark by an acquaintance of my father's led to my stay in Mr and Mrs Ron Pirie's comfortable house in a leafy suburb of Nairobi. A welcoming home-from-home from which I was able to explore the whole country: hitch-hiking here, travelling by third-class sleeper there, borrowing a car when I could I stayed with hippies on the island of Lamu, ran out of money in Mombasa and survived on sweetcorn and pineapple bought from street-vendors, went on a boat round Lake Victoria, watched big game in the bush, and got a car stuck in the mud beside some lions. Looking back, I wonder how I had the nerve to do it. Not the bumming around – I mean arriving to stay with people I had never met. Anyway, thank you Mr and Mrs Pirie, I hope I will be as generous if a layabout student lands on me some day.

A few years later I returned to visit my wife, who was in Kenya on a medical assignment. She was also staying in a well-appointed house in Karen, a suburb of Nairobi, but working in some of the city's most squalid shanty towns. On this trip I had an equally great time, marred only by coming down with some sort of dread African food poisoning on New Year's Eve. You may know the sort of thing. Stuff pours out of you from top and bottom – well, mouth and bottom to be more accurate – until you think you are going to die. This soon gives way to a feeling that you want to die, until finally, dehydrated and weakened, the conviction grows that you have already died.

The whole incident left me with an inferiority complex about my digestive system's ability to cope with foreign travel. It also raised question marks in my mind about medical practitioners. Each of the several doctors I happened to be with at the time had different suggestions as to what to do when I started to get ill, none of which did any good at all. As I got worse they all left me to my fate, apart from my wife who, if I recall correctly, prescribed Fanta lemonade to aid my recovery. Mind you, I may have been hallucinating by then, or possibly fantasizing.

Anyway, what it did not do was diminish my affection for Kenya. In the highlands, the cool hillsides and mountains provide a pleasant climate right on the Equator. In addition there are wide African plains, extraordinary wildlife, the spectacular Great Rift Valley, a fantastic coast-line on the Indian Ocean, tea plantations, forests, deserts and lakes. Kenya's population is an engaging mixture of black Africans from a variety of tribes, spiced with Arab traders at the coast, Asian traders in the towns, topped up with an intriguing collection of ex-pat and resident

ABOVE AND RIGHT: *The Mara Safari Club and the green green grass of Africa. In the river are dozens of hippos, in the tent running water and electricity.*

whites. It accords with my idea of paradise and so I jumped at the chance to go back there to make a documentary.

As it happens, I do not think my own experience of the country is particularly unusual. White people visiting East Africa have always gone looking for wildlife, the great outdoors, excitement and adventure, but usually manage to find some home comforts to fall back on. Karen Blixen had a farm in Africa, but like everyone else she had house-boys and farm-hands to do the actual work.

Like everywhere else, Kenya is not what it was. But some things never change. A generation or two ago white people went there as colonial administrators, big game hunters and missionaries. Now, thirty years after independence, they are UN representatives, photojournalists and charity workers. The same collection of do-gooders doing pretty well, and ne'er-do-wells doing even better.

The film was to be about the Maasailand. The Maasai Mara is a marvellous area of classic African grassland, dotted with acacia trees, lying about 150 miles to the west of Nairobi. Part of the Mara is set aside as a National Park which, with the Serengeti just across the border in Tanzania, constitutes an important area for African wildlife.

The Maasai people who live in the Mara – nowadays, outside the National Park – are semi-nomadic pastoralists who are just the sort of people to inspire awe and affection in British Empire-builders, anthropologists and modern-day tourists. More than most of the other tribes in East Africa, they have clung to their traditional lifestyle. This for them means avoiding such naff things as growing crops. The traditional Maasai life centres on herding cattle. The more cattle you have, the better you are doing. You drink cows' milk, sometimes cows' blood, and you eat cows' meat.

The Maasai have a reputation as being brave fighters. They have fought other tribes, fought the colonizers from Europe, and fought civil wars between themselves. What the Maasai have never done is kill the wildlife. A few lions have been engaged in mortal combat to prove bravery or to protect livestock. But the zebra, the elephant, the wildebeest and the antelope have been left alone, regarded as God's cattle. This has meant that in the Maasai area of the country the wildlife has continued to flourish, even outside the National Park itself.

But will this last? Over the last few years some of the Maasai have changed their ways and have started to see the advantages of the modern world of agriculture and money. Some groups, who usually own land in common, have sold or leased their lands to people of other tribes for use in agriculture. Other villages have taken to growing crops themselves.

In these areas, the herds of wild animals have ceased to be God's cattle, sharing the grazing with man's cattle. They have become pests, which threaten to trample the corn, ruin the harvest and steal the farmers' profits.

Was the Maasai lifestyle disappearing, and would the wildlife go with it? I headed towards the Mara to find out.

Up country

I drove to the Mara Safari Club in a Land-Rover, all the way from the nearby airfield, pausing only to draw a map of Africa in the earth for the benefit of the cameras. This I did with only the assistance of a stick and a printed map. Not only do I do my own stunts, I also do my own cartography.

The Mara Safari Club is one of the tourist resorts which are the modern epitome of the adventure-with-comfort philosophy I was referring to. It is outside the National Park. Ostensibly it is a campsite in which you are sleeping under canvas miles from anywhere, right out in the African bush. Strictly speaking, all that is true, but the tents are permanent fixtures, each with running water and electric light. They even have en-suite bathrooms. The food is excellent in a British sort of way. The camper's day starts when he is woken at first light by a waiter bringing tea and biscuits to the tent veranda. If he wants the biscuits, he has to hurry up and eat them or the birds will get there first. Off he goes on a game drive, a tour round the locality in a Land-Cruiser, his driver finding wild animals to look at, hopefully without too many other vehicles full of tourists round them as well. Back to the camp for a full cooked breakfast, then off on a late-morning drive to see anything he missed the first time round. A curry lunch taken outside in the hot sunshine is very acceptable, after which the afternoon could be spent relaxing by the swimming pool until it is time for afternoon tea. Then back out on safari at twilight and home again for early-evening drinks and a five-course dinner. The whole thing is not cheap but nor is it to be missed by anyone who is not roughing it on a real safari. On a real safari you go off on your own with only your driver, guide and bearers to help you.

The various lodges have slightly different styles. From a previous visit I remember Governor's Camp, which is in the Mara as well but inside the Park, being very impressive and slightly wilder. The Mara Safari Club is just a little over-fenced (they do not allow lions to wander in at night and kill the clientele as it is bad for repeat business). And it has what is

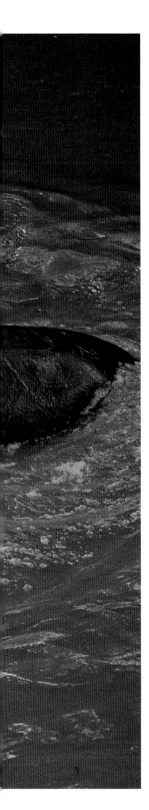

basically a crazy-paving path leading to the tents. Set in the close-cropped grass it is slightly too redolent of English suburbia. What it does have, though, are hippopotamuses.

The tents are strung along the banks of the Mara river, a squelchy brown watercourse which meanders around the edge of the camp. In it, 20 or 30 feet down the bank, live the hippos. Dozens of them. They spend the day wallowing in the muddy water. They are ideal animals to accompany tourists. Fat, ugly, messy creatures, lying around bathing all day. And the hippos are much the same.

I know it is wrong to judge animals on how they appear to us. Different species look the way they do because of the requirements of their life cycle. And they should not be praised or condemned on the basis of anthropomorphic aesthetic considerations. Having said that, hippopotamuses really are ugly. From the Greek, their name means river horse, but river pig would be more like it. They have hideously obese bodies, nasty pink eyes and mouths which they open wide to emit fearsome noises which are somewhere between a roar and a belch. If their hairless sludge-coloured skins were not enough to put you off, hippos have an unattractive way of emptying their bowels. As huge amounts of waste material emerge from their vast rear ends, they fan it with their tails, spreading it around the river they live in. The original shit hitting the fan, in fact. No wonder the water is so brown.

The hippos spend the whole day in the river, engaged in face-to-face yawning and snarling contests over their favourite stretches of the sluggish waterway. They have contests which threaten to get really nasty but never seem to develop into actual violence. Perhaps they are just discussing their royalties on the song that Flanders and Swann used to sing about them.

Oh, all right. I loved them really. I could have spent hours watching them wallowing in the muddy water. In fact, I think I did.

At night the hippos heave themselves out of the water and go off foraging for the huge amounts of food it takes to get them to full size. Come the early morning they grunt and groan their way back to the river, into which they dive with all the grace of Robert Maxwell falling off his yacht. You must be able to hear them miles away. You can certainly hear them yards away in your tent.

The hippopotamuses in dispute over rights to a particular stretch of river. This sort of thing goes on just yards away from the tourists staying at the Mara Safari Club.

In addition to the hippos along the river there is an occasional croco-dile, a giant floating lizard with malice aforethought. On the opposite bank baboons chatter and swing in the trees while a line of mongooses urgently go about their business. Weaver birds weave, fly catchers catch flies and kingfishers fish for kings.

There are different Creation myths, but personally I believe that when God created Africa, he was on drugs. The rest of the world does not have animals the size of dumper trucks wallowing in its rivers, so what was He up to with hippos? Stoned. The rest of the world has tall trees, but it does not, like Africa, have frankly ludicrous creatures like giraffes with unfeasibly long necks so they can eat the topmost leaves. The rest of the world makes do with squirrels, and monkeys and things which take the trouble to learn how to climb trees and so do not have to walk round looking like a street lamp inspection crane in fun fur. Rhinoceroses are, just like hippos, pointlessly large, but not so fortunate. Unluckily for them, they have been endowed with an impressive horn at the front, a quite unnecessary piece of decoration which is as pointless as the wings on 60s American cars. They eat grass, for goodness' sake. Why do they need to carry an offensive weapon around on their top lip? Rhinos have been hunted to the point of extinction because their horn is supposed to put a bit more lead into gullible Chinese pencils. And what about elephants? Who in their right mind would come up with another giant animal, this time one which can perform more or less every activity with its nose? I know God can do anything, but coke-head or what?

Female of the species

Having been filmed settling into my luxury bivouac, it was time to meet my translator and guide. For my benefit, someone had been hired who had spent years in this part of Africa, spoke Maasai, Swahili and several other languages, and who was used to the difficulties of life up-country.

When my old-Africa-hand arrived, she was something of a surprise. Carolyn Roumeguere is a beautiful, dynamic, French twenty-something who has had a particularly exotic upbringing. Her mother was a social anthropologist who came to study the Maasai and loved them so much she decided to leave her French husband to marry a Maasai Chief. She still shares her life with him, and he shares his life with her and the six other wives he has since acquired.

Carolyn was a small child when this happened and was brought up amongst the Maasai in their villages until she was sent to Nairobi to be educated in the ways of the Western world by an English governess. Later she attended university in Paris, earned her living as a fashion model, and now makes her money exporting jackets and jewellery to Europe. But she is most at home roaming around the plains of Africa. Not quite Saunders of the River, but someone you would genuinely want to go into the jungle with.

Don't fence me in

We set off to visit a village near Narok. Narok is the local big town, but it is a couple of hours' drive down the bumpy mud roads and tracks from the Mara. Even longer for us, since we had to stop from time to time to film the countryside we were passing through.

The open country of the Mara was looking very green. For several months there had been drought and the land had burnt dry, robbing the animals of water and then food as the grasses withered away. This is part of the annual cycle of events but droughts seem to be getting longer in Africa nowadays. But by this time the rains had come and the grass was putting out new growth. Dotted with trees, the fresh green shoots made the grass look like English parkland. This sort of scenery might well have appealed to British colonizers, but it was not so welcome to British film-makers. It is no good coming all this way if it is going to look like Richmond Park. Mind you, you do not see as many herds of wildebeest, zebra and antelope in Richmond Park as you do here.

As we got nearer to Narok the landscape changed. It was much drier, the rains had only really come to the high ground and, in place of bush country dotted with trees and circles of huts, there were huge open fields, fenced off, cleared of scrub and planted with maize. This did not look like English parkland – more like Canadian prairies. This was evidence of the change of use which is stealing over this land.

Near Narok we visited a Maasai village which had gone over to agriculture. A confident young man called Simon showed us round. I am not sure if he was the head man of the village, but he was clearly its spokesman. He was not by any means the oldest, nor was he the richest nor necessarily the bravest. He had his position because of his skills as an orator, a skill valued in Maasai tradition as in our own. Anyway, this village John Major was now the village's representative on Narok County Council and was dressed in a formal suit to welcome us to the village.

The village was a simple sort of affair with thatched huts strung in a line. Carolyn hurrumphed that it was not a proper Maasai village at all. The houses were the wrong shape and made of the wrong material. They

were not arranged in a circle and the place was messy. Worst of all, the village was surrounded by fields sprouting maize and other crops.

Simon explained that the village had gone over to growing crops because they brought in an income. Crops took them out of the subsistence-level life they had previously enjoyed. The main drawback they now experienced was trouble from wild animals. Elephants especially had a nasty tendency to break down fences and munch their way through a few acres during the night. What they did not eat they trampled underfoot. Elephants and other animals sometimes even killed people; Simon showed me a girl whose mother had been killed by a buffalo, and who was still awaiting compensation for her death. Ordinary people were not entitled to kill the wild animals which threatened their new livelihoods. That had to be done by the Kenya Wildlife Service (KWS). The KWS was responsible for preserving the wildlife and also protecting people from the wilder wildlife. But, according to Simon, although the KWS was quick to punish any poaching of animals, it was slow to protect the farmers from the marauding animals.

But did not the Maasai traditionally welcome the wildlife? And did not the wildlife attract tourists to the area? Simon was not interested in that argument. The animals should be confined to the Game Reserves, not allowed into his people's fields.

Thus this village had broken with its past, but not completely. The mothers of the village, including Simon's own very young-looking wife, gathered in traditional dress to sing me songs of welcome. They started with some religious songs and, goaded by my sadistic director, Simon demanded a response from me. So on an African hillside I launched into *Amazing Grace*. As soon as I started I remembered I do not have much of a singing voice. It did not take too long for it to become obvious to everybody else.

The mothers had more of their songs to sing. They sing as a group, with two or three lead singers backed up by ten or twelve others. Their voices have a whining haunting quality not unlike bagpipe music or a collection of Kate Bushes. This is a living tradition: they were not singing ancient folk songs but ones which were recently made up about topical subjects and matters of local concern. For example, they sang a song praising Simon for his efforts in arguing for the elephants to be chased

TOP LEFT: *Carolyn Roumeguere, my guide, was brought up with the Maasai. An African enthusiast, designer, model and fantastic linguist.*
LEFT: *The rhino is much in demand for its horn.*

away. This was all too up-to-date for me: I was racking my brains to think of a recent *Spitting Image* number I could belt out, but sadly I was not called upon a second time.

We were a bit gloomy during the long drive back to the lodge. Other people have no right to expect that the Maasai should refrain from taking the step from pastoralism to agriculture, just because of the romance of their traditional lifestyle. But it is sad nonetheless to see a way of life disappearing. There is something very attractive about nomadic people generally. Perhaps we respond to some atavistic urges lost within us. Perhaps it is their arrogance we admire. The Maasai were traditionally disdainful of other tribes which grubbed around in the dirt to produce food, but now they are literally being brought down to earth.

The rains fell as we made our way back the lodge on roads made almost impassable by the downpour. The roads are built of mud and round here mud comes in two forms – red, which is difficult to drive on when wet, and black, which is totally impossible. In the dark there are the further hazards of trucks which have skidded to a halt across the road and the odd baby elephant appearing in the headlamps. Baby elephants are not like the baby rabbits you might bump into in Britain. You cannot just drive over them. They are to be avoided at all costs, especially as they are usually accompanied by mummy elephants.

Somehow the driver of our 4x4 managed to get us home. Amazing when you think that these off-road vehicles are really designed for shopping in Knightsbridge.

Out of Africa

The next day Carolyn took me to a traditional Maasai village to see the real thing. It was easy to see how markedly the agricultural Maasai of the day before had departed from the ancient ways of the tribe. In this conventional village, or *enkang*, the houses were arranged in a circle enclosing an area the shape and size of a very large roundabout. Branches and bushes are arranged around it to provide a hedge. At night the cattle are herded into the central enclosure through the three or four gaps between the houses, which are mainly joined together in groups of five or six, forming short, curved terraces. As a result, the ground within the village is covered with squished-down cow dung which forms a soggy, springy floor for men and women to walk on, and children to play in. The Maasai generally go bare-legged, wearing brick- or blood-red blankets. Perhaps this is why. A central plaza of cow dung seems weird at first but it is surprising how quickly one gets used to it, and to the flies.

Cow dung is central to the village physically and central to village life generally. The houses are low single-storey huts made of wood plastered with cow dung. The roofs were not the pitched roofs of the previous day's village but rounded and slightly convex, made also of cow dung. Cow dung, even when dried, does not sound like the perfect roof covering but the night before there had been rain of monsoon-like intensity and the roofs in this village had not been washed away or sprung any leaks.

It struck me that the restaurant and bars at the lodge, which are permanent buildings, have roofs decorated with a straw thatch to make them look authentic but really they ought to be covered in cow dung.

We were invited inside these genuine houses and, indeed, filmed inside one where I was welcomed by the woman who lived there. Filming was not easy as the space is limited and there is very little light. The houses do not have windows as such, just one or two little openings to let some daylight in and some smoke out. The smoke comes from an open fire which is used to heat the house (scarcely necessary on the day we were there) and to cook food. Smoke from the wood fire hangs around inside until it can find one of the little openings to slink out of.

The Maasai set great store by their milk. It is collected in a calabash, a misshapen bottle sized container made from a hollowed-out gourd. We thought it would be good fun for me to drink the milk from a calabash, but when it came to it the woman who was kind enough to give me the milk insisted on pouring it into a glass first. The milk has a slightly smoky, herby taste imparted by the inside of the calabash which is cleaned out and, I hoped, sterilized by burning embers.

A calabash is also used to collect cows' blood. The jugular vein is punctured by an arrow and sealed afterwards with cow dung. Thus the Maasai are able to milk their cattle of blood without having to kill them. But, as it happens, I was not offered cow's blood to drink. Luckily I had ordered gold top, not red top.

Certainly, a glass of Maasai milk on its own was not enough to turn me into a Maasai. That, in their highly structured society, is a long job. Boys go through several stages before they reach full status as an elder of the village. At puberty the boys are lined up to be circumcised in public. This is obviously painful (it can take up to five minutes) but the idea is

OVERLEAF: *At home with the Maasai.* LEFT: *The traditional house is constructed with cow dung walls and roof.* RIGHT: *Cooking is done at a wood fire inside the house. Smoke escapes from small holes in the walls and roof.*

not to cry out in pain or call Childline or anything. Crying is a sign of cowardice and takes some living-down afterwards. The boys then become *morans* – young warriors. They grow their hair long and smear it in red ochre. *Morans* are supposed to go off into the bush, kill lions, steal cattle and do a whole lot of other things, most of which are next to impossible in the modern world. *Morans* are heroic figures who enjoy a few years of excitement before they are ready to come back to the village to marry, settle down and become elders.

Girls are also circumcised at about the time of puberty. Female circumcision, which is a feature of many peoples around this part of Africa, is somewhat of a euphemism, as it involves rather more radical surgery than the removal of the male's foreskin. The girl is held down while her clitoris and labia minora are cut away. The girls are at least allowed to undergo this ritual in private and are not obliged to refrain from screaming in agony while it takes place.

Lost in admiration for Maasai life as I may be, circumcision for males or females strikes me as a very strange practice. I wonder who first came up with the idea. *Hey, guys, never mind inventing the wheel, let's cut bits and pieces off our bits and pieces. In fact, let's do it to all our children … Then they can do it to theirs, and so on to the end of time …*

I had always understood that female circumcision was fundamentally intended to suppress a wife's enjoyment of sexual intercourse in order to discourage unfaithfulness. This, however, does not seem to accord with what actually happens in Maasai society. Men are allowed to have more than one wife, but it is also accepted practice for a woman to take lovers. She is not supposed to choose them outside her husband's age group, but otherwise she has a free hand. All the children she bears are always accepted as offspring of her husband, although it is preferable to have at least some who resemble him more than his chums. Girls and boys have sexual intercourse from a young age, although it is considered bad form for an uncircumcised girl to get pregnant.

Most of this I discovered from talking to Carolyn or doing background reading. In a spirit of enquiry I tried raising questions of sexual behaviour with the Maasai women themselves while sitting inside the cramped quarters of the village house we were filming in, but I was given precious little information. But then, being squeezed into your own home with some complete strangers and a camera pointing at your face is not conducive to intimate disclosures in any culture.

What I did establish was that each house has two beds fixed into position on either side of the fire. The mother sleeps in one with her children, unless she is being visited by her husband or a lover. Anyone else who may be in the house sleeps in the other. I am afraid I did not stay the night to check all this out.

Some of the older villagers remembered Carolyn from her early days in the district and berated her for still being unmarried. To what extent, I wondered, had Carolyn been inculcated into the life of the Maasai in the raw? As a small girl she told me, she had been held down and a couple of (milk) teeth pulled out, which is the standard East African way to ensure a channel for feeding in the event of lockjaw. But that was the worst thing that had been done to her.

How genuine was all this? Forewarned of our arrival, the village mothers had given us another sung greeting (puzzlingly, none of our team was asked to sing on this occasion) and on display was a variety of spears, clothes, jewellery and other Maasai trinkets which the villagers sell to tourists.

The Maasai used to enjoy a ferocious reputation. Their belief was that all cattle in the world belonged to them, so stealing cows from other tribes was not larceny. Was the choice open to them either to abandon all their old ways, or to preserve themselves and some traditions as living curios, pale imitations of a once-proud race?

We considered the problem over our pre-dinner drinks back at the lodge. Pre-dinner entertainment consisted of half-a-dozen waiters and security guards dressed in all the finery of *morans*. They danced in the high leaping style of the Maasai warriors in a very impressive and convincing way. But their long red ochre hair was false – wigs put on to give us cocktail drinkers an idea of what Maasai life is like. Maasai life is a cabaret, old chum.

Live and let die

The next day, a cynical city slicker called Maina Mwangi told us we were mad to worry about the Maasai way of life. Maina is an Oxford-educated Kikuyu (the dominant Bantu people of Kenya) from Nairobi and has no time for any sentimental noble savage stuff. As he put it, nobody comes to Africa to take his photograph, but he is as African as any Maasai. They are going to be pushed aside by inevitable changes, just as English rustic life has changed over the centuries. And just because he is Kenyan does not mean he is in love with African animals. Quite the reverse. If he wants to see wild animals (which is rarely), he is happy to see them in the zoo.

We appealed to the romantic side to his nature. What about the magnificent herds of animals? What about the culture which was

LEFT: *The Maasai favour red – the colour of blood.* TOP: *Traditionally, they regard all cattle as belonging to them.* ABOVE: *Maina Mwangi shocks Carolyn by suggesting that Kenyans could happily do without their wildlife.*

disappearing? What, once the animals were no more, about David Attenborough's TV career? Maina remained unmoved and suggested that the sooner the Kikuyu farmers moved into the area the better.

We told him that the animals are a unique resource, able to attract tourist revenues, whereas crops are duplicated the world over, and in the long-term likely to turn the plains into a dust bowl. Overall, it was a risk he was prepared to take. Humans come before animals. Whatever the economics dictate, that is the route to be followed, and the Devil take the hartebeest.

We could have gone on chewing the fat much longer, but there was a danger that Carolyn might have strangled him.

Pachyderm patrol

At the moment there are still animals in Kenya, and farmers. And trying to keep them apart is the job of the Kenya Wildlife Service (KWS). If farmers are not to be allowed to kill the wild animals, then the Wildlife service must prevent the animals interfering with agricultural land. Elephants are emerging as the main cause for concern so we arranged to tag along with a KWS patrol to see how they scared elephants away.

We set off at about four in the morning with a detachment of eight KWS men led by their officer, Joyce Wafula. She explained that foraging elephants would come out of forested land during the night and make for maize fields, generally taking the crop just before it was ready for harvest. As dawn came up they would retreat into the trees. To frighten the herd off cultivated areas, first find your elephants. This is not quite as easy as it sounds, as they do drift away pretty quickly. It is impossible to track them at night, and they keep in the trees in the full of the day, which is why this scaring-off tends to be done at first light.

Joyce took us to an area which was divided up into *shambas,* smallholdings worked by individual farmers. This was Maasai land which had been leased to members of another tribe. The earth was suitable for crop growing but because it was surrounded by forest and bush it was liable to constant encroachment by elephants. In fact, if Maina will forgive me for saying so, it was the humans who were doing the encroaching because, until the farmers moved in, this had been part of the elephants' range.

Farmers in England have trouble scaring crows away. An elephant is even less likely to be put off by Wurzel Gummidge. Once you have found your elephants you have to put the wind up them with explosions, thunder-flashes and gunfire. In this way you can frighten more elephants than you can shake a stick at. Since they are intelligent animals they should begin to associate the farmers' fields with the nasty bangs and decide to stay in the uncultivated forest for a bit of peace and quiet. Unfortunately, their intelligence means they eventually notice that the explosions, thunder-flashes and guns are not actually hurting them so from time to time you have to kill one or two, *pour encourager les autres*.

With the patrol we made the important discovery that it is possible to lose a herd of elephants in a matter of seconds. They are well-camouflaged against the tree trunks and move very fast when they want to. We might have got close enough to the herd to worry them a little, but certainly nowhere near enough to film them. It was nonetheless great running full-stretch across the rough ground trying to keep up with the fit young men of the KWS, who were trying to keep up with the fit old elephants.

We decided we could not give up as easily as that and set off to track the elephants through the woods. How difficult can it be to stalk elephants? The KWS employ all the techniques of animal tracking that I had learnt with the 4th Harrow Weald Scout Troop. Techniques which had proved to be so utterly useless in suburban London, but which were invaluable here in Africa. Elephants leave very shallow, dinner-plate-size footprints on the ground which are fairly easy to spot when:

(1) you have understood the configuration to look out for and
(2) there is a KWS patrolman standing next to one and pointing it out to you.

Then there are the branches and bits of grass, which are bent over in the direction that the elephants travel. To spot these you really do need to be a member of the KWS. Being a Boy Scout Patrol Leader (Retired), I can report, does not help at all.

And finally there are elephant droppings to go by. These are substantial at the best of times, but particularly so – elephantine, in fact – when the elephants are scared by pursuing humans and on the run, so to speak. To make sure you are close behind the elephants you have to check that the droppings are fresh. The easiest way to do that is to stick your finger in the dropping to take its temperature. If it has gone cold the elephant is long gone. If it is still warm, the elephant cannot be far away. If it is warm and getting warmer, the elephant is probably standing over you and still doing it.

After several hours of elephant-tracking we realized it was totally pointless as the elephants knew we were after them and were perfectly capable of keeping out of range. But I can recommend a day's walk in

the Kenyan forests. It was not jungly and overgrown with creepers – in fact it was rather like a walk in Sherwood Forest but with no danger of coming across CenterParcs. If there was any danger from animals or snakes, all I can say is the KWS did not mention it.

Elephant man

The next day we tried again, this time with more success. We were able to surprise a small group of elephants at the edge of some woods. The KWS chased them this way and that, while the director chased me this way and that, hoping to get me near the herd and on-camera. Since both the elephants and I were convinced we were going to get our faces blown off by the explosives, we actually found ourselves going in the right direction from time to time. I do not know if all these shock tactics keep the elephants away, but I did not go back again.

One problem we had with filming this sequence came from our government minder. Peter was a townie himself and when he first joined us he and his city clothes looked a bit out of place in the bush. In supervising us on behalf of the government, he did not interfere with our activities except to object vociferously once when we accidentally went off to do some filming without him. This threatened to be a problem until we were able to smooth things over with him. By the time of the elephant run, he had rather got into life in the great outdoors. Reluctant to stay in the background he insisted on keeping up with the KWS and me. I mention this in case, when you watch the documentary, you notice amongst the muted greens and khakis a figure in a bright red tracksuit and inappropriate loafers. That is Peter.

Magic lantern

Back at the Mara Safari Club, I attended a lecture by their resident naturalist. This took the form of an old-fashioned illustrated lecture given by the appropriately bearded and well-informed Mike Clifton. From him I discovered that the Maasai had not merely tolerated wildlife, but their activities actually encouraged it. If left alone, the plains in the Mara would gradually become overgrown by a tough grass which absolutely nothing can eat. In the absence of human activity this would choke out

PREVIOUS PAGES: *Maasai regard game as 'God's cattle'. Now, elephants threaten the livelihood of those who have taken to agriculture.*

the other grasses and plants, and even bushes, considerably reducing grazing for the wild herbivores. After several years there would inevitably be a fire. The tall dry grass would burn ferociously, scorching the earth which would then take years to recover. The Maasai land management involved burning off this grass on a regular basis when it was much shorter. The set fires would cause much less damage to the land and ensure better grazing for the cattle and the wild herbivores alike.

Mike also described the massive migration of wildebeest which takes them up and down Africa, in and out of the Mara and the Serengeti. I had seen this sort of thing many times on television, but I had not before understood that zebras have a strange way of joining the migration, appearing to supervise and control the very stupid wildebeest as they cross rivers and other obstacles. *Don't risk going over the river on your own. Always use a zebra crossing.*

And why do zebras have stripes? Mike Clifton suggested that their markings do not make them invisible to predators such as lions but that very possibly they put off the tsetse flies, whose multi-faceted eyes are disturbed by stripes. I made a note that next time I am in Africa I must bring a wardrobe of Newcastle United shirts and pin-stripe suits.

Up in the air

But is there any future for the Maasai and the wildlife?

One possible way forward has been identified by an organization snappily called the Ol Choro Oiroua Wildlife Management and Conservation Association. My next step was to meet Willie Roberts, the Association's Executive Director. Willie is a white Kenyan who lives in a private camp a mile or two down muddy tracks from the Safari Club. Originally he came to this area to farm but became disillusioned with the steps you have to take to keep wildlife off farmland. He tried electric fences, but the elephants learnt that the fence posts were not live and so would trample them down. He tried staying up all night to scare the elephants away, but the human flesh weakened before the elephant spirit wilted. He was advised to kill a couple of elephants and drag their bodies around the boundaries to put the smell of death about the place. It was at this point that he decided there must be a better way.

The key point that he and the Association realized was that the move towards agriculture was being hastened because the landowners around the National Park – the Maasai themselves – were earning little or nothing from tourists who came to see the wildlife, but could earn quite a lot by turning their land over to agriculture.

LEFT: *Willie Roberts, farmer turned environmentalist, likes nothing better than some dare-devil flying in his plane.* ABOVE: *I had a bath in Africa. Willie's permanent campsite has an elegant outdoor bathroom. My time there was spoiled when I was grabbed by the paparazzi.*

Of course tourists do pay to come to this area – they pay a great deal, but the money earned in admission fees and taxes is collected by hotel-owners, the national government and local government. If the Maasai landowners received the proportion of this tourist revenue to which they were already entitled, they would have a direct financial interest in the survival of the wildlife. And there would be much less pressure to enclose the land for crops.

In the Association are Paramount Chief Ole Ndutu and other Maasai landowners, Willie himself and a Nairobi lawyer called Stephen Mwensi. They operate what they call a Group Ranch scheme. Various owners pool their resources and so control a sizeable area of land. With the benefit of Stephen's legal advice they have been able to pursue a variety of court actions in order to ensure that they receive their rightful cut of the tourist revenue cake. If their scheme is successful a number of problems are solved. The Maasai can continue to raise cattle in their traditional way, live in harmony with the wildlife, but still receive an income equal to or more than what they would earn by going over to crop-growing.

From the conservationist's point of view, obviously the more land that is left for wildlife the better. As Willie explained when I chatted to him at his camp, the wildlife cannot live on the National Parks alone. The animals have to roam large areas in response to changes in the weather and the availability of grazing. The animals are unlikely to be given more land for their exclusive use, so it would be folly to get rid of areas where man and beast can get along together.

Willie's camp epitomizes the joy of the white settler's lifestyle. He and his wife have a large living room which, although it is covered by a tent, could be a comfortable sitting room anywhere in the English-speaking world. Sleeping-quarters are a string of other tents. In addition there is an extraordinary outdoor bathroom. Surrounded by a wooden palisade is a free-standing Victorian bath which has to be filled with water heated by a wood-burning stove. It is Robinson Crusoe made over by *Homes and Gardens*. Naturally I had to have a bath in these unusual circumstances. The water is as brown as the water in the River Mara, as is the water in my bath at the lodge. Mud in the water is probably good for you, but is there just a whiff of hippo?

Naturally I could not persuade the director to leave me alone, and the cameraman crept up on my bathtime, trying to catch me playing with my rubber crocodile.

As the night fell at Willie's camp I sat round the campfire listening to the lions roaring in the woods. All creatures great and small can be glimpsed or imagined in the African bush. The next morning, across the lawn came wart hogs to feed on the scraps which are put out for them as though they were blue tits. No wonder Willie loves it here and has given up trying to be a farmer.

Willie has a dry sense of humour which came to the fore when he took me up in his light aeroplane so I could see the change in land use from the air. He has being flying for decades in a sort of gung ho way that leaves you slightly in doubt as to whether his improvized repairs will keep you in the air. As he demonstrated his aeronautical skills he seemed slightly disappointed that his diving, banking and looping were not making me feel ill.

'Not sick yet, Clive?' was his merry cry as he went into another turn. Not me. If only he knew – one taste of underdone chicken and I would have been finished for days.

Willie was depressed as he showed me the encroachment of more and more shambas into previously open country. Even more worrying are the large fields of commercial proportions. It is extremely doubtful whether this tropical, indeed equatorial, environment can sustain the clearing, ploughing and soil disturbance that it takes to grow cash crops. Near-desert can turn very easily into near-disaster. In the 30s the Americans managed to turn their Great Plains into a dust bowl by over-grazing and over-farming land which had supported roaming herds of buffalo for time immemorial.

Here and there are fields on which farming has been abandoned, and the bush is making an attempt to reclaim the land. If it is successful, perhaps the wildlife will find its way back as well.

It is equally obvious from the air that tourism puts its own strain on the land. Tourist buses keep going even during the rainy weather and leave ugly tyre marks over the soggy ground as they track and circle the big animal attractions. Sensible management and control, confining tourists to set areas, and building roads, would help preserve the land, but that would make the place even less 'wild'.

But Willie and the Association are convinced this is the way forward. Who disagrees?

Well, the reason it is so important to include the lawyer in their set-up is that the Association has had quite a legal battle with Narok County Council to obtain its share of the tourist money. More than that, the Association has been asking what has happened to the money the Council has collected over many years. Are there hospitals and schools which have been built with the money? Where are the accounts?

This mixture of money and politics, with just a suggestion of corruption, is as potent a brew here in Kenya as anywhere else.

Party political

Kenya has done pretty well since independence in 1963. Very well, compared to the other countries in the region. If you consider the disasters and upheavals which have befallen the Sudan, Uganda, Rwanda, Burundi and Ethiopia, the stability of Kenya is remarkable. As a democracy it is far from perfect. Its great first leader, Jomo Kenyatta, turned the country into a one-party state. His likely successor, Tom Mboya, was assassinated in 1969, simply, it is widely assumed, because he was not a Kikuyu. His actual successor, Daniel Arap Moi, has ruled very firmly, and had to counter an attempted *coup d'état* by the Air Force in 1982. In elections held in 1992, his success was assisted by the simple device of doubling everyone's money just before polling day. The inevitable inflation developed only afterwards. Had they stuck with a Westminster-style democracy, of course, he would instead have had a pre-election tax-cutting budget and engineered a mini-boom, but there you are. Still, to most people, Kenya is the acceptable face of capitalism in Africa.

But politics can be a rough old trade in rough young countries. And a doughty battler on the political scene is the Honourable William Ntimama. And the Association have him to contend with.

William Ntimama was the Chairman of Narok County Council for a while before joining the cabinet as Minister for Local Government, a position he has held for several years. The title Minister for Local Government conjures up the picture of a rather anaemic figure. John Gummer, perhaps, crossed with Gillian Shepherd. In the flesh, the Kenyan Minister is much more robust and partisan than that: Michael Portillo out of Ian Paisley.

He agreed to meet us on a Saturday when he was going to be in his constituency, Narok North. He mentioned he would be meeting some constituents, and we imagined this was going to be something like an MP's surgery. In the event it was a large public meeting with some of the qualities of a royal garden party.

William Ntimama's fine house has a substantial garden with an area of lawn the size of a school sports field. When we arrived, the garden was full of hundreds of his political supporters. Town councillors, elders

PREVIOUS PAGES: *Flying over the Maasai Mara. From the passenger seat of Willie Roberts's plane, I could see the changes in land use as the Maasai begin to cultivate the land around their villages.*

of the community, women in traditional dress, and anybody else who wanted to come and 'pay homage' to the Minister, as he put it in a casual aside to me.

Several hundred of the guests queued up to greet their host and a few of his close associates. I was invited to join the receiving line, like the bride's father who happened to turn up at the last minute. Older people shook hands with us. Actually, the custom here is to touch hands, as I noticed only after I had crushed the fingers of the first twenty people in the line.

Children and young people bowed and presented their heads to be touched. This is standard Maasai etiquette for showing your respect to anyone old enough to be your parent, a system which works fine in a society where age is venerated, but which might cause havoc in Hollywood. Imagine the clash of heads between Joan Collins and Elizabeth Taylor.

At the end of the greeting process Ntimama was presented with a couple of goats. Politicians clearly do better here than in Britain, where the best they can hope for at a constituency gathering is a piece of rubber chicken.

Later on, Ntimama addressed the crowd in the Maa language of the Maasai. One of his daughters, who were home for the holidays from an English public school, languorously translated parts of his speech for me. The daughters were dressed like Maasai princesses but spoke like Sloane Rangers. They had obviously seen Daddy in action before and were not going to get excited by a few people who had come for Saturday lunch on the lawn.

Ntimama is evidently a good orator. Speaking off the cuff, his jokes and remarks went down well with the crowd. As well they might. Poking mild fun at us, 'some white men who were interested in wildlife', along the way he said the Maasai should be able to expand their population if they wished. Birth control was unnecessary as they were only recovering lost ground. He also said it had now been declared that, if an animal kills, it shall be killed. The Maasai did not want to finish the animals off but did seek to prevent the animals finishing them off.

He also expressed great delight about the removal of Dr Richard Leakey as the head of the Kenya Wildlife Service. This referred to a very public, very bitter feud in which Ntimama had led a campaign against Leakey, the world-famous environmentalist and palaeontologist. Although respected internationally, Leakey's forceful style had made him many enemies within Kenya, none more ferocious than Ntimama. One Kenyan magazine likened their feud to a battle between two elephants.

In effect, Ntimama puts himself forward as a leader of the Maasai people. The Maasai have genuine grounds for complaint. However admired they were as noble savages, they were excluded from the development of the country in colonial times and many have continued to be left out of things since independence. As with other tribes in Kenya, some of their lands were taken by white colonizers. And as with other nomadic people, title to their land has sometimes been difficult to maintain against the more organized claims of settled people. National Parks, land set aside for animals, have made further inroads into the area available to them and, understandably, furthered their resentment of animal conservationists, especially those from abroad who have not preserved natural habitats for wildlife in their own country.

This well of anger is exploited by Ntimama, and his outrageous, inflammatory remarks both in and out of Parliament have made him notorious in the Kenyan Press and in political life. What he embodies, though, is the argument that the Maasai should compete in the modern world with the other tribes in Africa. They should seek material improvement in their conditions by moving away from a 'primitive' lifestyle as noble savages. I suppose it could be argued that it is more noble to be a farmer growing your own food than to become an exhibit in an African theme park. Ntimama, though, is not totally against wildlife tourism: he is part owner of the Governor's Camp Safari Lodges in the National Park.

After his speech there were songs from the women of a succession of villages. As before, the women were in traditional dress. Their orange, red and white cottons and intricately beaded necklaces were in bright contrast to most of the men who were in duller, more Western clothing. The whole event was a powerful combination of old and new, ancient tribal loyalties being deployed in pursuit of modern political ends.

I sat on a low bench with dozens of elders and councillors (including Stephen from the agricultural village). Ntimama sat on a chair which had been ceremonially carried out into the field.

Ntimama was eventually free to be interviewed. He laughed off my suggestions that he was being controversial in his speech, inviting people to have babies and kill elephants. No, he said, he was a politician and had to speak in sound-bites to attract attention. He was in favour of

TOP: *The Honourable William Ntimama greets young people with the conventional Maasai touch on the head. Hundreds of people came to 'pay homage' to him on the day we were filming.* BELOW: *A Maasai elder at the meeting.*

the Maasai improving upon their milk-and-blood diet and going into agriculture. He was concerned about the two years of drought this part of the country had suffered, but did not think the farming they were now doing was likely to turn the area into a dust bowl.

I had understood that he was very much opposed to the Association's group ranch schemes, fighting tooth and nail to protect the interests of the Narok County Council and its revenues. But on-camera he expressed affable support for their efforts, although he thought other ranches closer to the National Park might do even better. He cheerily agreed that the Council should be publishing accounts dealing with the revenue it had received, and said that they probably would be doing just that in the not too distant future.

His bark on this occasion was much less worse than his normal sound-bite.

End of the road

My time in Kenya was coming to an end. There was a little time left for me to take a proper look at the wildlife. Despite the anxiety for its future, there is plenty to be seen.

I practically ran over a herd of elephants when I was being filmed driving through a thunderstorm. A family of cheetahs, a mother and three young females, took up residence just by our lodge. As is their way, prides of lions sat patiently in open ground ignoring any vehicles which come to watch them digest their food.

Ol Choro Oiroua are even seeking to reintroduce rhinos to their area. They have a bad-tempered pair which they have imported from South Africa ready to release into the wild. But at the moment they are being kept safe from poachers with a round-the-clock guard. Perhaps more than anything they symbolize the future, because so much of the natural world now only exists with the protection of mankind. There is no wilderness left.

Finally at the lodge I interviewed Paramount Chief Ole Ndutu in company with Willie Roberts and Stephen Mwensi. It is odd that the way forward for this part of Africa might be found in an alliance between an

PREVIOUS PAGES, LEFT: *The Maasai who gathered at Ntimama's home are determined to engage fully in the modern world, but they still dress and decorate themselves with extravagant beauty.*
RIGHT: *The pride of Africa.*

old Maasai Chief, a farmer turned environmentalist and a smart city lawyer.

Ndutu is an old man and in poor health, but still has the energy to worry about the future. One way or another, one cannot help thinking that the Maasai way of life is on its way out. If encroaching agriculture does not destroy it, money from tourist revenue will. Many young Maasai are already employed in Nairobi as security guards, protecting rich people from burglars, rather than their own villages from lions.

Chief Ndutu could not be sure that in fifty years' time there would still be Maasai herdsman tending their cattle in the Maasailand, but he was confident there would still be lions chasing wildebeest. In that, at least, I hope he is right.

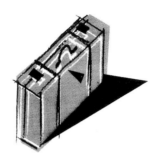

Our Man In...

TIMBERLANDS

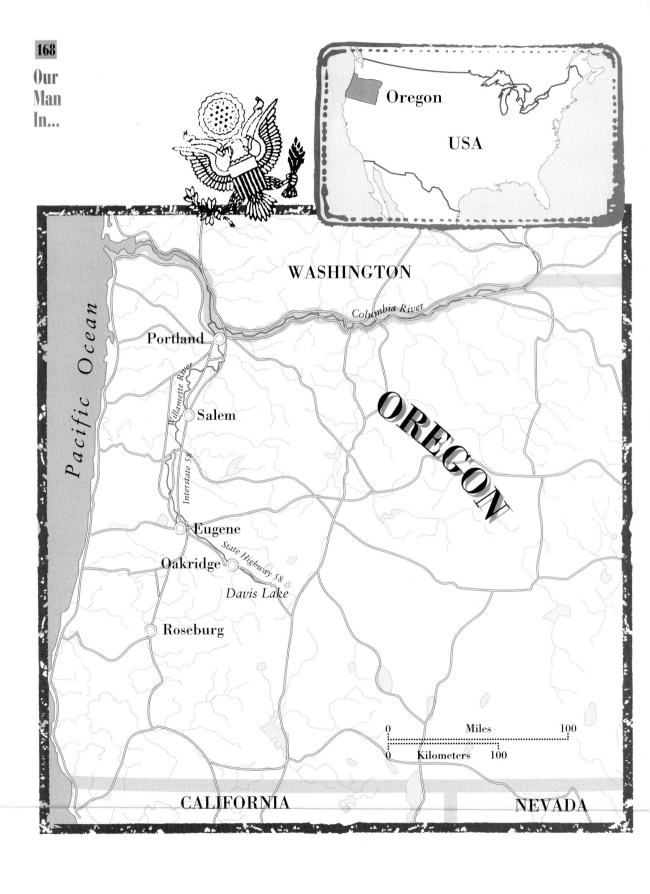

Oregon

USA

WASHINGTON

Columbia River

Pacific Ocean

Portland

Willamette River

Salem

Interstate 58

Eugene

State Highway 58

Oakridge

Davis Lake

Roseburg

OREGON

CALIFORNIA

NEVADA

0   Miles   100

0   Kilometers   100

WHEN Europeans first started arriving in North America they must have found it astounding. A whole new continent with hotter summers, colder winters and wider open spaces than anything most of the tired, poor, huddled masses had left behind in the Old World. Here was a New World full of natural resources just waiting to be explored and exploited by anyone in pursuit of a better life or a quick buck. In many ways it was a paradise. True there were Red Indians living there already, but it was relatively easy to push them aside. Not to say slaughter, corrupt and betray them. By hook or by crook, the Land of the Free was not going to remain the Home of the Braves for very long.

The modern map of the United States reflects the path of the European immigrants. On the Eastern Seaboard there are twiddly little states like Connecticut, New Hampshire, Rhode Island and Maryland, with boundaries which take account of the topography and history of their area. But as the pioneers went westwards they could not be bothered with all that and drew straight lines on the maps with rulers to mark out great blocks of territory in the shape of oblongs and squares which eventually became fully paid-up member states of the Union.

For my visit to Timberland I was going west to the end of the Oregon Trail, which is, of course, Oregon. In the 1840s the Oregon Trail, a notional route across the country, brought land-hungry homesteaders to the far North West, lured by the promise of free land. The American government offered 640 acres to each man who cared to claim it. Later this was amended to 320 acres for each man, plus an extra 320 acres if he was married. There was nothing at all for a single female. This was a subtle inducement to matrimony. Many preferred to head south to the gold fields of California, but in due course Oregon attracted enough settlers to establish it as the thirty-third state of the Union.

Oregon (which is known as the Beaver State), is an area of mountains and rivers and lakes, but above all an area of trees. The trees are big round here, and so is tree-felling. Oregon has lived off its mainly coniferous forests – Douglas fir, spruce, cedar, pine and hemlock – for one hundred years. Some of the trees have been here for much longer than that. But environmentalists are worried that too many ancient woodlands have been chopped down by the timber industry, and that such tree-felling has to stop. And they have decided to use every means possible to prevent the ancient forests being destroyed, enlisting in their support the Northern Spotted Owl.

And so I set off on the trail of the beaver, the Spotted Owl and the lonesome pine.

Go West, young man

Salem is the state capital of Oregon, and Portland is its largest city, but I was heading somewhere nearer the trees – the logging and university city of Eugene.

Eugene is a pleasant, home-town kind of place. Like most American home towns, when you first get there it seems kind of empty. Everything is spread out, as you might expect from a place which started with everyone being issued with 640 acres apiece. Mostly it seems empty because of the motor car. In America nobody walks much from A to B unless A is where he is now and B is where he left his car when he got here.

America has drive-in cinemas, drive-in banks, even drive-in wedding chapels, and, of course, the drive-in hotel, the motel. Motels still exist all over the States, motels just like the one in *Psycho,* only, with any luck, nothing more distressing is waiting for you in the shower than the remains of the previous occupant's soap-on-a-rope.

The motel I checked into in Eugene was the Parkway Inn, two floors of basic hotel rooms alongside a convenient parking lot. No restaurant, no bar, just the bare essentials: a bedroom, a bathroom and a TV set. Pizzas you can have delivered.

The manager of the Parkway was called Troy. He had longish blond hair and black-framed glasses. He did not look like anything out of *Psycho.* In fact he looked like Garth out of *Wayne's World.* Troy was real friendly and he was very much at home in the Parkway. He does not get paid a fortune by the owners of the joint, but that does not stop him lavishing upon it all the care and attention of a fanatical do-it-yourself home improver.

Troy's pride and joy is the 'Love Room'. It has a heart-shaped bed, a heart-shaped doorway and a heart-shaped Jacuzzi. Bright red plaster cupids fly above the bed. It is built for that romantic night with the woman of your dreams. In case the woman of your dreams does not turn up in person, there is an extensive selection of pornography to watch on the television to help you make it through the night.

Duty calls, however and I had to bone up on trees. By coincidence, there was an item on the local television station, KMTR, about the conflict between environmentalists and the logging industry. Actually it was not particularly fortuitous, as this is the big issue round here and KMTR covers it more or less every night.

The latest bulletin announces that the Greens have come up with a few more animals and plants whose existence is said to be threatened by logging in Oregon. The Northern Spotted Owl has always been on the list but now it has been joined by the Marbled Murrelet (a bird, apparently), the Short-Nosed Sucker (don't ask), the Red Spotted Pocket Mouse, plus a selection of newts, bats, voles and other critters. Plus some crazy stuff called wild parsley, which I assumed was something you might add as a garnish to magic mushrooms.

The loggers, meanwhile, have found an academic who claims that more of Oregon is covered by trees now than it was one hundred years ago. I did not hear much more about him during the rest of my visit. He sounds exactly the sort of person that would get a column in *The Sunday Times*.

The next morning I decided to check up on the story at KMTR. I also decided to check out of the Parkway Inn, and check in to the Eugene Hilton.

KMTR is housed in a neat but rather anonymous building on the edge of town. An introduction is reasonably easy to arrange. Everyone has heard of the BBC. In fact, it is quite amazing the number of Americans who claim to watch nothing but BBC programmes on America's non-commercial Public Broadcasting Service (PBS). With such massive popularity, you would think that PBS has the biggest viewing figures in the country instead of languishing, as it does, somewhere between the 24-hour weather forecast and the shopping channel. Also, it has to be said, the classy BBC productions that Americans particularly love generally turn out to involve Benny Hill. It has been my sad duty to inform dozens of Americans that Benny Hill is no longer with us. (He left the BBC years ago and life on earth rather more recently.)

Anyway, Jim Brown, the deep-voiced newscaster at KMTR, whose set I wandered on to at the end of another Oregon update, said I should check out the rendezvous that Earth First! was holding that weekend up in the Deschutes National Forest. If I went there I could get the story from the environmental activists' point of view. He told me to be prepared to eat lentils and take a tent. Jim Brown appeared to be charming and sincere. Appearing to be charming and sincere are, of course, the major subjects at American newscasters' school (along with nodding your head now and then when speaking on camera *and* emphasizing *the* wrong words *in* a sentence). But I thought I could act on his advice.

It was the sports correspondent who was the real delight. After giving the baseball scores and the results of the High School Athletics Meeting, he stood up to reveal that, although his jacket and tie were visible above the desk, he wore nothing but a pair of shorts below. Benny Hill would have been proud.

Drive time

Earth First! is a nationwide group of environmentalist activists who have an annual get-together in the Oregon Forests, and they were to be found by the side of the Davis Lake, which is just down the road from Eugene. This being America, 'just down the road' means getting on for 100 miles away. The road takes you through Oakridge, which is exactly what a town way out west ought to be called, alongside the Willamette River, which is not exactly what a river way out west should be called. It sounds more like a character in an Australian soap opera – 'Charlene, have you heard? Shane has left Draylon and run off with Willamette. I think she must be pregnant!'

In fact, the Willamette is the principal river of Oregon. Here and there it has been dammed to form reservoirs which are now part of the very fresh-looking landscape of water, woods and hills: Scotland without the mist, Austria without the people. The road, however, is pure Americana. American roads go on forever. Along them drive enormous American trucks which go on forever as well, axle succeeding axle, bearing loads the size of Liechtenstein. They are great. But American cars leave me cold. They have pointlessly large engines, soggy suspensions, ghastly plastic interiors and a complete absence of style. Detroit car-makers deserve all the trouble they get from Germany and Japan. Yet American trucks are unbeatable. Chrome-plated radiators, chrome-plated exhaust chimneys, chrome-plated bonnets, chrome-plated chrome. An American truck cab is a work of art, a truly regal throne in which sits the king of the road, the truck driver.

The truck driver is the all-American hero, travelling all over America, heroically keeping open the arteries down which flows the life blood of Uncle Sam. While heroically clogging his own arteries with fried food bought at the ubiquitous McDonalds and Wendys and Taco Bells.

The timber trade makes its contribution to the highway. Twenty tree trunks the size of, well, tree trunks are hauled down from the hills into the lumber yards in great big articulated trucks. The trade is supposed to be threatened by the environmentalists but, even so, great Birnam Woods travel to their Dunsinanes every day in impressive lorry-loads.

In fact, ordinary cars are a rarity along these Oregon roads. The Oregonian driver prefers to travel in a pick-up with a weird roof, trailer or other bespoke customization. Fashionable at the moment are monster-mobiles with high, fat wheels to lift the chassis several feet off the ground. Perhaps *Mad Max II* has just hit the state? Those heading for the hills travel by 'recreational vehicles'. These giant motor caravans allow you to take everything – including at least two kitchen sinks, a lavatory, air-conditioning, television and sound system – as you drive off to get away from it all. 'You can't take it with you' may be true of life in general, but it is not true of the American holiday-maker in particular. A crash between two of these movable monstrosities would keep a Third World shanty town in household equipment for ever.

Lunch is eaten in a roadside diner in Oakridge. It has everything. Fellow diners are characters out of *Twin Peaks*, all denim dungarees and weird-looking eyes. You cannot tell if they are gentle, sad country folk or serial killers. There are no red necks in these parts as everyone wears their hair short at the front and long at the back – the early 80s style kept alive in England by Ian Botham.

The waitress cracks gags for all the world as if she were in an American road movie as we order. I plump for an elkburger, made from real local elk. Very edible but bland. Exactly like a hamburger, in fact.

In fact, exactly like 99 per cent of American food. Nowhere else in the world are you offered so many different choices of foodstuffs, all of which taste of nothing at all, unless you cover them in the sauce of your choice, in which case they taste of sugar and salt. Travelling in a large party makes ordering fast food a slow process. Selecting your main course is just the start of it. A meal always comes with side-orders and add-ons. By the time each of you has specified the type of bread, the type of salad, the type of salad dressing and the type of coffee, you have forgotten what it was you ordered in the first place.

After a two-hour snack we had to press on to the lakeside rendezvous. We turned off Interstate 58 and on to a couple of back roads, then on to a forest track. We were on our way to meet a group of people who were desperately worried about the loss of trees, yet all we could see were trees, mile after mile of Christmas trees, conifers, pines, spruces.

Now, I love trees. Old English oaks, Brazilian rainforests, palm trees, shoe trees, all of them. My credit card even supports the Woodland Trust. But at first sight these conifers are just a touch boring. Growing straight up, they lack character. Telegraph poles with a garnish of green leaves.

Was this the forest that they were trying to protect, or the plantations which were replacing it? The brightest feature of some of the roads was the bright yellow flowers of the European broom. They call it Scotch

OVERLEAF: *Davis Lake, the venue for the Earth First! rendezvous. They claim that it has shrunk because of climatic changes brought about by tree felling.*

broom round here, where it is regarded as a pest. Introduced from, presumably, Scotland, it threatens to take over the whole place as its seeds lie dormant for years, ever ready to spring up as soon as land is cleared. Nothing seems to kill it, and it is displacing native species. Revenge on America for the grey squirrel, perhaps?

Wood stock

There was no sign of any Earth Firsters along the empty forest tracks until at last we came across a very orderly line of parked vehicles. There were about fifty of them, all parked tidily on the one side of the road. These people were supposed to be anarchists, for goodness' sake. Had they no sense of disorder?

You could tell they were not hunters or fishermen because of the bumper stickers – *Save the Forest; Save the Owl; Save the Whale; Save the Bumper Sticker; Nuclear Power, No Thanks; No More Roads; Kill your Television.* If a car did not have one bumper sticker like that, it had several.

The cars all appeared to be about ten years old. Perhaps the theory is that cars get more environmentally friendly as they get older?

In the woods, the Earth Firsters were getting organized in a non-organizational way. In the absence of a hierarchy, orders were being given and received on a voluntary basis only. We met Tim Ingelsbee first. He is not the leader of Earth First! There are no leaders. But he does talk to the media quite a lot. He is tall, gentle and determined, and he knows what he is talking about. Equally importantly, his long brown hair braided into plaits provides an ideal frame for apocalyptic sound-bites about the destruction of our planet through big business and bad management.

Earth Firsters were getting things set up for their weekend. Groups were forming to have teach-ins and seminars on nature studies, law, sex and sexuality, that kind of thing. Here and there were supplies of food and a lot of fresh drinking water in plastic containers. Not ecologically sound but, hey, at least you stay alive.

For the weekend, hippie dress is the standard clothing for the environmental activist: ponchos made from old army blankets for the men, long flowery skirts and monkey boots for the women – the hempen homespun uniform of the disaffected radical the world over.

As we strolled by the lake, Tim talked me through his concerns. Since the White Man came to the North West United States (and Canada, for that matter) he has been steadily working his way through the trees. As well as forests cleared for agriculture and housing, tree-felling for the timber industry has been gradually cutting into the naturally occurring woodland, the rate of destruction increasing since the war and the introduction of the chain saw. In theory, the timber industry replants as it goes along and, of course, given time, the forest can regenerate itself, but in practice the environment has been seriously damaged. Commercial pressures on corporate owners of private land force them to maximize their profits as fast as they can, so they tend to fell as many trees as possible as quickly as possible. The Federal Government owns a great deal of land from which it sells the timber on a regular basis. It should act more responsibly than private owners and to some extent does, but even in these Federal forests, the call of the mighty dollar rings out loud and clear. Politicians are not immune to the blandishments of big business and the desire of voters to keep their jobs.

When it comes to replanting, the diversity of the original forest is usually replaced by the single fastest-growing species. The result is what Tim calls a tree farm. It is not a real forest which has a mixture of ancient and modern trees of different species and supports countless other plants and animals as well.

The industry's preferred method for extracting timber is to clear-cut, which means to remove all the trees from a substantial area. This looks very ugly when it has just happened and can cause serious long-term damage. If you remove the trees completely the subsoil gets washed away by heavy rainfall. The streams get clogged with mud and the salmon die off (causing job losses further down the river). If enough subsoil is washed away the trees cannot grow back at all, and you have created a desert. No good for the environmentalist, and no good, in the long-term, for the logging industry either. Nowadays the loggers do not touch the trees which grow beside the streams and rivers, in order to help retain the banks and aid the recovery of the land. But would they have done that without the pressure exerted on them from environmentalists?

Since ultimately they both want to protect trees, there should be plenty for the loggers and the greens to agree on, but in fact they are at loggerheads. Earth First! claims Oregon is down to the last 5 or 10 per cent of old-growth forest. But the loggers dispute this and reckon that quite enough land has been set aside as wilderness already. They are worried about losing their jobs – and, indeed, their whole industry – if

OVERLEAF: *Tim Ingelsbee is every inch the environmental activist, his hair and moustache framing eco-friendly sound-bites for the media.*

muddle-headed concerns about imaginary threats to the environment unnecessarily prevent legitimate use of a renewable resource.

Earth First! makes the point that the wilderness areas are the least productive for man and nature. It says that there is no point in continuing to cut down the old woods to the very last ancient tree. The industry would come to an end then anyway, so you might as well stop before you have spoiled the land for good.

Tim is used to arguing these points with the logging industry, and in the media. But this weekend there are no arguments. He is camping with the converted. Earth Firsters have all the virtues – and vices – of hippies, Friends of the Earth, Woodcraft Folk, Luddites and Boy Scouts rolled into one. In fact, they chiefly resemble religious fanatics. Earth First! is a pantheist faith believing that the Earth as a whole is of far greater importance than mankind. Like religious zealots, Earth Firsters preach higher moral standards and foretell Doomsday. Unless we mend our ways Armageddon will come as rivers are poisoned and the ground is turned sour by our sins of commission and pollution. Or something like that. The End, at any rate, is Nigh.

Unlike most religious zealots in America, Earth Firsters are regarded as highly subversive. I chatted to a woman called Judi Bari. She was able to walk, just, with a stick. A bomb had gone off in her car when she was organizing protests against the cutting of redwood trees in California. To add insult to injury, literally, while she was recovering in hospital she was charged with being in possession of the bomb when it was in her car, just before it exploded and smashed her pelvis. The charge must have been based on the suggestion that she was going to plant the bomb somewhere herself, but she denies this and is convinced that someone in the timber industry was out to kill her, and that the FBI were out to frame her. Can things really have got this serious?

This weekend, though, is a retreat and a chance to commune with nature. Lake Davis is 4000 feet above sea level. Its area has shrunk over the last few years – the rainfall has lowered because of the reduction in tree cover, Tim tells me – and therefore has a flat area of land covered in springy turf alongside it which used to be part of the lake bed. From here the view is of hills covered with woods, one or two mountain tops covered with snow, and the remains of some ancient volcano still covered in solidified lava. However much tree cutting has gone on since they arrived, it must have been just this sort of landscape that the White Men gazed upon in wonder when they first got here.

'To make it complete, some Indians should come swooping down from the hills,' I remarked to Tim.

'No, we are the Indians,' he replied, somewhat delphically.

After nightfall there is a campfire. The plan is to film me chatting to people as they gather round the flames, but getting permission to do so is not easy. Some Earth Firsters have apparently had nasty experiences with television reporters. In any case a TV camera epitomizes the world of consumerism to which they all object. But the chief problem is that there is no leadership as such, no formal structure at all. All Indians and no Chiefs. (Perhaps that is what Tim meant.) So no person or persons can give permission on behalf of anyone else. Asking a group of fifty people whether we can film is a process fraught with difficulty. Eventually we establish the idea that we will be filming and anyone who does not wish to be caught on-camera should keep out of the way. That seems to be acceptable to most people, but one petulant voice demands:

'Hey, what if you don't want to be filmed, but you do want to hang out by the fire?'

In the end we were allowed to film. A certain amount of fat was chewed, breeze was shot, and toss was argued. A couple of guys started playing their guitars and a couple of girls stripped to the waist. We did little to establish whether their environmentalism was merely a fashionable stick with which to beat the consumer society or a real breakthrough in political thinking. Most concern was expressed at the shortage of beer. The guy who was organizing it was apparently engaged in ecological discussions with his girlfriend in a distant tent.

In the darkness a voice asked me, off-camera, what my real views were on Earth First! I had been warned that FBI agents infiltrated the organization so I went carefully, even though the questioner was from New Zealand. Well, I evaded, I have only just got here, I do not know enough yet to make up my mind.

'I thought you guys in Britain would have done massive research before you arrived,' my questioner sneered.

'I thought New Zealanders were polite,' I tried as a riposte.

Some other voices, not knowing that I was still there, roundly abused the BBC as our crew bus drove off. It was time for bed.

The camera crew were off to stay in a warm hotel back in Oakridge. But to get the full flavour of a night in the woods, and to retain credibility with the Earth Firsters, I was sleeping under canvas. While it was light I had pitched, with the maximum of fuss for the cameras, a Hillary bell tent which I hoped was named after Sir Edmund Hillary, the first man up Everest, rather than Hillary Clinton the First Lady in the White House. Now that it was night and pitch dark, it was difficult to find the tent. It was not far from the lake, near some trees, a description which would

ABOVE: *Early one morning just as the sun was rising. The tent is named after Hillary, the first man up Everest, not Hillary, the First Lady in the White House.* TOP LEFT: *It all looks very silly but Judi Bari was crippled when a bomb exploded in her car when she was involved in a tree cutting protest.* LEFT: *It was cold in them there hills, but the Earth Firsters gathered around the camp fire for a sing-song.*

apply to no more than 1000 square miles of this continent. It had been quite a cold day and threatened to be an even colder night. Why was I doing this? It was by no means certain that the tent was even waterproof. Television programmes are normally made in nice warm studios with a quiet dressing room beforehand and hospitality afterwards. I wanted to win a BAFTA, not a Duke of Edinburgh's, Award. Did the director (himself on his way back to Oakridge) secretly want me to get frostbite in the documentary?

In the event the night was not too bad and I managed to survive it with a sleeping bag for bedclothes, a Barbour for a ground sheet and a warm researcher for company. The only interruption during the hours of darkness came from some revelling Earth Firsters playfully attempting to let the tent down. No real malice, just a test of our good sportsmanship, which was rewarded with a bottle of Jack Daniels. So at four in the morning I found myself teaching the night visitors games from *Whose Line Is It Anyway?* which eventually drove them back to their own tents.

Next morning the scene was magical. The subtle grey of the early morning sky blended with the pastel colours of the hills to be reflected in the still water of the lake. The cry of the occasional bird flapping over the lake's surface rang out as clear as a bell from half a mile away. I was one of the first up but gradually the voices of other early-risers could be heard celebrating the dawn. I had not been camping like this for more than twenty years. I decided I must do it again. In perhaps another twenty years' time.

I picked my way through the trees to find the carefully dug latrines. The campers here were radical, anarchist hippies to a person, but Baden-Powell would have been proud of them. Everything here was done exactly as set out in Scouting for Boys. I wondered if there would be Church Parade on Sunday.

My thoughts having wandered to and from the Relief of Mafeking, I awaited the arrival of my troop to record for posterity my early-morning awakening in this corner of paradise. This was duly filmed at about 11 o'clock when they made it back from their corner of bed and breakfast luxury in civilization, the cameras capturing the moment when I emerged from my tent on the way to lunch.

This morning everyone seemed friendlier. Perhaps it was because I had shared the experience of one night in the open with them.

My next interviewee was a very committed activist called Peg Millett. In fact she had been committed to prison for two years for taking part in an activity called monkey-wrenching.

This does not involve monkeys but does involve literally throwing spanners, or monkey wrenches, into the works of industrial activity thought to threaten the environment. Monkey-wrenchers reckon that if you vandalize or otherwise interfere with the actions of big business you will be able to render unprofitable certain economic activities you disapprove of.

The best-known example of monkey-wrenching in the tree-felling business is to hammer metal spikes into tree trunks. A hidden metal spike in a tree can wreak havoc with the sawing equipment at a sawing mill. At the worst it can threaten the lives of mill workers, at the least it might require every tree to be X-rayed before it is cut into planks. At any rate, the very threat of these metal spikes makes the lumber industry less profitable. Monkey-wrenchers get up to other activities as well, including the removal of markers in the forest set up to show which trees have been sold at auction. They block drains on forest roads built to allow access for heavy equipment, hoping that a big storm will flood the road or even wash it away.

These methods are all set out in a book called *Ecodefense,* edited by Dave Foreman and Bill Haywood. It is printed on recycled paper, naturally. But also with soya-based ink. I am ashamed to admit I have no idea what ordinary ink is made from. It isn't seal cub blood or anything nasty like that, is it?

The First Amendment to America's Constitution makes it impossible to prevent the publication of a book which manifestly encourages illegal activity. In Britain you could probably only publish it if the words were removed and dubbed on later by an actor speaking in an Irish accent.

Anyway, whether or not she had been encouraged by the book's methods, Peg Millett had been convicted of destroying an electricity pylon in an attempt to disrupt uranium mining in Arizona. She was caught when a friend she had known for years informed against her. It turned out that the so-called friend had been an FBI agent all along, and had only got to know her to turn her in to the authorities. Sometimes you just don't know who to trust.

Woodman spare that tree

An area which throws the dispute between the conservationists and the loggers into sharpest relief is Warner Creek. In October 1991 a fire swept through about 9000 acres of prime Spotted Owl habitat on which tree-felling had been banned. The fire stripped the trees of every leaf and twig, scorched the earth and killed all the wildlife. Presumably the owls flew

ABOVE AND LEFT: *Warner Creek's trees were killed by a massive forest fire, but it remains at the centre of a debate between environmentalists and the timber industy.*

away. Only the tree trunks remained standing, blackened and unbowed, but dead.

Tim took us to the creek. It is an eerie place. The blackened trunks of thousands of dead trees stand where they perished. If left alone they would remain upright for many decades. The fire here has acted like a neutron bomb and destroyed all life while leaving the structures in place.

All the evidence indicates that this was a man-made fire. Tim is convinced it was arson deliberately committed by loggers. This may seem like paranoia, but there are some grounds for his suspicion. Although the area has been destroyed as a forest, the wood in the trees would still be usable if it were removed. Indeed, the logging industry has pressed for the right to extract the timber now that the area has been ruined anyway. Conservationists make the point that whether or not the fire was started with this end in view, to allow logging now would be an open invitation for loggers to set fire to inconveniently protected areas all over the country. The loggers are incensed that there is good timber here which is just going to waste. And so we are back to the fundamental difference between the two sides. To the logger, a tree which falls down and rots away is an utter waste. To the environmentalist, a tree which rots is part of the life cycle of the forest. So even dead tree trunks should be allowed to sink slowly back into the ground.

To me, dead trees standing on a blackened hillside look like a bad result for everyone. The baby chopped in half before Solomon has given judgement.

I am not a lumberjack and I am not OK

To speak to the loggers we went to see Wilbur Heath who used to run Heath Logging. Actually, he still does, but now the company is called Mountain Resource Management. Wilbur, a giant redwood of a man himself, wryly acknowledges that his activities have had to be renamed. He is no longer clear-cutting sections of the forest, but engaged in 'view enhancement'; his business is no longer called logging but conducting 'ecosystem management'. He is not chopping down trees but 'harvesting renewable natural resources'. His parody of politically correct language, although a joke, does represent a victory for environmentalists. Their concerns are now setting the agenda.

But Wilbur claims that the loggers are the real environmentalists. He says the so-called environmentalists are preservationists – they do not want to see anything altered or used for the benefit of mankind. Be they environmentalists, or preservationists, they do seem to be winning many of the battles. The Endangered Species Act was passed in 1972 to conserve threatened wildlife by, amongst other things, protecting their habitat. In the modern American way, a steady stream of legal actions has identified more and more species dependent on the forest. And so it has become more and more difficult to chop down trees.

The Northern Spotted Owl is the most famous, or notorious, of these protected creatures. Wilbur says the 1972 legislation has been unfairly exploited by environmental groups who seek to bring to an end to logging, which was never the intention of Congress when they passed the Act.

Nor are the owls completely innocent. Wilbur reckons they are cleverer than most people realize. He says one of their favourite prey species is the tree rat, great numbers of which are brought to earth by tree-felling. Owls are therefore attracted to areas where tree-felling is taking place. Consequently it always looks as though there is a high population of owls in areas where tree-felling is occurring. Tree-felling is thus blamed for destroying the owl's habitat.

To Wilbur, this is madness. He argues that the trees are a renewable resource. In that sense, the timber industry is not like coal mining or oil extraction. And even with the best growing methods there are about eighty years before a crop of trees is harvested, which should be quite long enough for the natural world to enjoy them. In addition there are wilderness areas set aside which are not interfered with at all. Wilbur's main ire is directed at Earth First! which he regards as a smelly, slimy terrorist group. The book on eco-terrorism has not gone unnoticed by people like Wilbur who have invested their lives in logging and their money in logging equipment.

He showed me the work which is done by him and his men. The men prefer not to be called lumberjacks. They say 'lumberjack' is a Canadian term. Or maybe it was the Monty Python song that put them off. They are tree-fellers.

The actual business of tree-felling is relatively straightforward. First you use a chain saw to cut into your tree on the side you want it to fall, until you reach about the middle. Then you cut in from the opposite side until the tree topples over, perhaps helping it in the right direction with a wedge or two, hammered into the trunk with the blunt side of an axe. As you reach the point when the tree cannot hold itself up any longer, there is a sad creaking noise – the death cry of a king of the forest, or two bits of wood rubbing against each other, depending upon your sensibilities. This is followed by a resounding crash as a magnificent specimen hits the ground or a depressing splat if the tree turns out to be rotten.

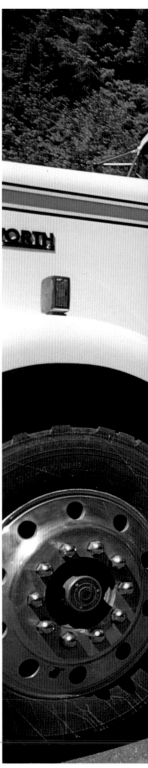

On the forest floor, the trunk is trimmed of branches and cut into 30-foot lengths. The whole process takes a matter of minutes. While this part of logging cannot be anything like as physically demanding as it was before the invention of the chain saw, it is clearly no work for a wimp. You have to watch out for the tree kicking back as it keels over and bringing you to the ground with it. You must be careful not to massacre yourself with the chain saw. And you need a sure foot to pick your way over the damp ground strewn with felled trees and branches all tangled up with the undergrowth. Getting the trees to fall in the right direction is made to look easy by the tree-fellers. The only stage I was allowed to help with was to shout 'Timber!' when a tree was about to fall. They really do shout 'Timber!' when a tree is coming down. Unless there are environmentalists around, in which case they shout, 'Hey, you like trees! Why don't you stand over there and see if you can catch this one?' They are uncomplicated folk, genuinely puzzled by the opposition to their going about the forest doing an honest day's work for an honest day's pay.

Tree-felling has a simple charm, but getting the logs out of the forest and loaded on to trucks is epic. At the edge of a forest clearing, Wilbur Heath's men have positioned an enormous tower which forms part of a temporary funicular railway. A wire stretches about 80 yards from the tower into the recently denuded forest. Workers attach chains to the 30-foot sections of wood which are dragged down the hillsides by the engine which runs along the wire to the tower.

Once there, the logs are detached and then picked up one by one by a mechanical grabber, a lobster from the land that time forgot. Its metal claws are directed skilfully by its driver, who stacks the logs neatly on the back of an eight-axled truck which then drives down the specially built forest road to town.

The whole process is noisy, dangerous and impressive. Real man's work. Even the various engines involved must, you feel, run on testosterone. It is work that belongs to a time when man went nobly into battle with the wilderness. Has too much of the wilderness vanished? What will Wilbur Heath do with his logging equipment if there is no logging left?

PREVIOUS PAGES, LEFT: *Timber! Another one bites the dust.*
RIGHT: *These magnificent specimens are tree trunks being brought down from the hills in an equally magnificent truck. The driver is called David Anderson (probably no relation).*

Much the same question faces Jim Hallstrom. He is the owner of the Zip-o-Mill in Eugene. Here seasoned trees, when they can get them, are turned into planks of wood. Trunks travel along conveyor belts towards giant saws, like so many James Bonds left for dead by a sadistic baddie.

The mill is working on trees bought three years before. Since then, timber sales have been held up in a legal gridlock. Or perhaps that should be log jam. The Clinton Administration has tried to work out a compromise between the environment and the economy. (They had got to Option 9 at the time of my visit to Oregon.) But that would allow for only 20 per cent of the former levels of timber extraction from Federal forests. Better than the zero option which has applied for three years, but still likely to be disastrous for the little mills like this one which depend upon government timber sales. And disastrous for employment in the state of Oregon.

The mill used to employ more than one hundred people, but now that number has dropped to fifty. Of the six mills that were in the immediate area, Zip-o is the only one still in operation. The remaining workers are kitted out in blue denim dungarees, wear baseball caps and eat their lunch from tin boxes. They look the way American blue-collar workers have looked since the early days of the Flintstones. It is difficult to see what they would do if the mill ground to a halt.

Mert Minges who lives out on the Oakridge Road used to be a logger and did very well for himself in a small way. But his sub-contracting business was too small to survive in these difficult times, and his logging equipment lies rusting beside his single-storey wooden house.

He still uses his chain saw. But nowadays he uses it to carve wooden statues out of tree stumps and logs. Mostly he does bears, about 3 or 4 feet high. They are pretty good. Even when he shows you how he does the delicate work with a tool designed to hack through a trunk as fast as possible, you cannot really see how it is done. He can carve all sorts of forest animals and he knows exactly what the bears and the racoons and the elk look like because loggers, these so-called despoilers and destroyers of the forest, actually love going there. All of them go there to hunt and fish and enjoy the natural world. It is strange how much loggers and long-hairs have in common.

Mert blames the clamp-down on sales of timber from government land on the owners of private land who have felled their own forests in the reckless pursuit of profits. Mert is lucky because he has his skill as a chain-saw artist to fall back on, but he would rather be logging. In the meantime he is carving out a niche for himself in the economic environment.

Spotted Owl spotting

The niche that the Northern Spotted Owl has carved for itself is a highly inconvenient and irritating one for the logging industry. A breeding pair of owls needs about 1000 acres of roughly two-hundred-year-old Douglas fir forest in which to live. The owls nest in hollows at the tops of the trees and feed on the various vole, squirrel and other mammalian species which live lower down. They tolerate a few bare patches of ground and some young trees, but they have to have plenty of tall old trees. The dark dank forest keeps them cool in summer and protects them from the snow in winter. Of course, 1000 acres of ancient Douglas fir is exactly what the logger is desperate to get his hands, and his chopper, on as well. So the identification of the owl as a protected species has made it public enemy number one amongst the logging community.

Most of the loggers I spoke to claim they have never spotted a spotted owl in many years of working in the woods, so I assumed it must be difficult to track them down. Actually, it is very easy. All you need to do is go to the right stretch of forest with the right guide. We went to a protected woodland with Frank Oliver of the Bureau of Land Management.

How does the Bureau of Land Management differ from the US Forest Service? Well, I am not absolutely sure. One is so used to thinking of America as the land of free enterprise and unbridled capitalism that one can forget it has a bewildering array of bureaucratic agencies, departments and offices regulating and controlling all aspects of the American dream. The US Forest Service is basically part of the Department of Agriculture and seeks, so its critics would have it, to assist the exploitation of the forests for profit at the expense of a work of nature. With the Bureau of Land Management, which is more like an arm of a ministry of the environment, it is the other way around.

Anyway, Frank Oliver knew how to attract owls. You make an owl-like call near one of their nest sites and take along a supply of live mice. Immediately we arrived in the woods we saw an owl sitting on a branch. It recognized Frank's call and was licking its beak at the prospect of a few bite-size rodent snackettes (hold the salad). We got really excited and insisted on filming the owl from every angle, anxious that it might fly away before we had got some decent footage.

The Northern Spotted Owl stares enigmatically as the debate continues on the need to protect its environment.

Frank clucked at us and said film crews were always like this and not to panic, the owl would not be going anywhere. The owl is a placid, trusting kind of critter. It is not put off by film crews in the slightest. An avian Tony Slattery, it is happy to appear on television at any time.

For the mice it is less fun, more like a snuff movie. A mouse is put on a twig which you hold out in front of you and the owl makes its way down from the tree tops, flying from branch to branch until it is within swooping range of the unsuspecting little mammal. Released from its carrying box, the mouse has just started exploring the sights and smells of a real twig when the owl suddenly glides in and silently grabs it with its claws. It flies on to another branch and bites the mouse's head off. Nature red in beak and claw. Where is Ted Hughes when you need him most?

Both the male and the female owl are there, the male sometimes sharing his mouse with the female and she flying right to the top of the tree to feed her young. We could see the two youngsters way above us, sticking their heads out of their nest.

Spotted Owls are easy to film and easy to study. Researchers attach little radios to them to track their movements. They have no real enemies. Even their rather dodo-like trust in human beings has not been abused by hunters. The one risk to their survival is their dependence upon a natural habitat which has been steadily eroded and now requires elaborate protection to keep it in existence.

Trouble at Mill City

The Lesser Spotted Owl may have found its salvation in the Endangered Species Act. But is the genuinely endangered species now the lesser employed lumber worker? For the last part of the film we headed up to Mill City, whose very name celebrates its link with logging.

On the way there it was striking to see what a remote part of the world this is. Backwoods, in fact. It is a long way from Washington where vital decisions are taken; and it seems light years away from New York or Los Angeles.

Everything around Mill City is built on wood. And it is built from wood. Its public lavatories are wood-panelled. Everyone has wooden houses, so they have a rather temporary air. You feel that, in the event of an Indian uprising, their homes could still be formed into a circle to resist attack.

In the town's Trio Tavern the locals gather for a beer and to crack jokes about Spotted Owls and interfering middle-class hippie activists who cannot see the wood for the trees. The tree-huggers have ruined trade. And taken over the White House. The drinkers in the tavern were loggers and drivers and mill workers, all worried about losing their jobs. An Englishman, very popular in the bar and who now sells garden furniture, tells me he was the original drummer with Status Quo. He got out of rock music after the group's first hit, as he did not think they would last. I wonder if he keeps in touch with Pete Best? Naturally, he is in favour of leaving things the way they are. Surprisingly few of the regulars were actually born in Oregon. Until a few years ago Oregon was still attracting people from elsewhere in America. But not any more. Nobody comes here looking for work now.

Everyone wishes things could return to the way they were. Good old boys remembering the good old days. The problem for Oregon is that people cannot go any further west in search of a living. It is a worry for those who want to work in the forests and for those who want to save them. For everybody, this is the final frontier.

Opal Creek, made to make your mouth water

One way to stir things up in the Trio Tavern is to mention George Atiyeh. As a boy he spent a great deal of his time in Opal Creek, a virtually unspoiled piece of ancient woodland a few miles from Mill City. His cousin's grandfather owned the mining rights to the area and for many years prevented the Forest Service moving in and cutting down the trees. On the old man's death, George took up the cause and, through a friend's company, has acquired the mining rights which, under nine-teenth-century laws designed to encourage the extraction of natural resources, allowed him to fight and win many legal battles to preserve rather than destroy the environment. George has been a student, a playboy, a logger and a pilot. He is a bit of a sixties hippie, but very well-connected. Quite apart from his rich college friends, his uncle used to be Governor of the state.

To get to Opal Creek we drove along the road built by the Forest Service years ago when it was trying to get access to its trees. Once we reached the gateway we rode the rest of the way on horseback.

The mountain track takes you through trees which are hundreds of years old. One is said to be one thousand years old: a Douglas fir which was growing before the Norman Conquest of England. In the valley flow the crystal clear waters of the mountain streams. Here and there are the boarded-up entrances of old copper, zinc and gold mines. And at the centre of the reserve is Jawbone Flats, a collection of old miners'

ABOVE: *George Atiyeh shows me the way to Opal Creek and the way
to ride. The little girl is his daughter.* RIGHT: *Replanting the forest:
I do my bit.*

wooden houses occupied now by George, his friends and employees and therefore equipped with TVs, CDs and PCs, but from the outside looking just like the set of a Wild West film.

Opal Creek is available to scientists and students who want to come and understand the workings of a more or less virgin forest. There is a modern (wooden) building with reception rooms and bedrooms for visitors. During the winter the whole place gets snowed in but in the summer months it is a pure delight. Hydro-electric power provided by the fast-running river lights and heats the place: an environmentalist's heaven.

The only blot on the landscape is waste matter from some of the mine workings, but plans are in hand to clear that up. Ironically, although it is George's intention to keep the whole area in as pristine state as possible, he does have to continue mining activities so he can maintain his claim to keep the Forest Service off the land.

George may be a hero to the environmental movement, but in his own local community he is a pariah. One man's saved tree is a lot of other men's lost jobs. As George himself points out, they are decent folk around these parts but they are not above uttering death threats when they are riled. It happened to him so often that he even changed his answerphone message to encourage anyone making a threat to speak up if they were nervous about doing it for the first time. 'Leave your name and number, I *will* get back to you.'

People have refused to drink with him, or talk to him – he is the Salman Rushdie of Timberland. In the noble tradition of the Wild West he has come through it all to earn grudging respect from the local community, mixed with absolutely unbridled hatred.

It is a shame that it takes so much effort to preserve such a delightful place. North America is so huge that it is extraordinary to think there might not be enough room for places like Opal Creek. And room to cut and grow trees for fun and profit.

It may well be that the hatred of the environmentalists is simply a focus for the loggers' frustrations. Whatever happened, they would run out of ancient forest eventually. Unemployment, so it is said, would have hit the logging industry because of mechanization and competition from other parts of the world. So possibly the loggers are barking up the wrong tree.

Ingeniously, the logging industry argues that it is much better for the global environment if they are allowed to cut timber in Oregon, where replanting always occurs after trees are chopped down. If logging is stopped here, demand for wood products will not suddenly cease in

America. That demand will be met with trees in other parts of the world where replanting practices are likely to be much less strict. Ironically, logging will probably have to continue if only to supply paper for the mountains of reports, studies, legal case papers and books which the issue generates.

My last act before leaving was to plant a tree on some clear-cut ground. Everybody wants trees around here, be they logger, environmentalist or owl. For comic effect I accidentally drove over my sapling as I headed home. But have no fear. I planted another tree alongside it. In fact, no tree suffered in the making of the film: even the one I drove over bounced back immediately.

Maybe there is some hope for the future of trees in Oregon after all.

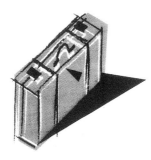

Our Man In...

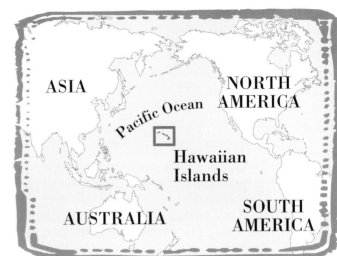

ASIA

NORTH
AMERICA

Pacific Ocean

Hawaiian
Islands

AUSTRALIA

SOUTH
AMERICA

THE HAWAIIAN ISLANDS

0   Miles   100

0   Km   100

KAUAI

OAHU

NIIHAU

Schofield Army Base   Honolulu & Waikiki

MAUI

Pearl Harbor   MOLOKAI

LANAI

Pacific Ocean

KAHOOLAWE

HAWAII or
BIG ISLAND

Hilton Waikoloa

Kailua & Keahole-Kona Airport

Captain Cook Memorial

Kealakekua Bay

OF the six places I visited in this series, Hawaii must be the one which most closely conforms to the notion of paradise. It consists of a group of sun-drenched, tropical islands, lost in the warm waters of the world's largest ocean. In your dreams, you may or may not have visited Hawaii, but you have certainly been there while listening to *Desert Island Discs*.

As it happens, I was not anticipating perfection. High-minded visitors usually report that Hawaii's indigenous beauty has been overwhelmed by the United States of America, into which it has been incorporated. Hawaii's native charm, they say, has been destroyed by the large numbers of non-Hawaiians who either settle or holiday there, while its remoteness ensures that, nonetheless, it is still an expensive place in which to live. Overwhelmed, over-populated and over-priced, it has long acquired the reputation of a paradise lost to all but the rich and tasteless.

It is certainly lost to Native Hawaiians. Two hundred and fifty years ago they had never met anyone from beyond the seas. One hundred years ago they were still a sovereign nation ruled by their own royal family. Now firmly under American control, pure-bred Hawaiians account for somewhere between 1 and 4 per cent of the total population. Even so, there is a political movement which seeks independence for Hawaii, possibly by way of reinstating the old monarchy. Hawaii for Hawaiians. Why not? It was certainly worth a trip to paradise, however tarnished, to find out if it could be done.

End of the Earth

The Hawaiian Islands are in the middle of the Pacific Ocean, a long way from anywhere. They are 2000 miles from the American mainland, 3000 miles from Japan and 4000 miles from Australia.

Human occupation was a recent innovation to Hawaii. It was first populated in about AD 500 when Polynesians finally found their way there during their steady migration through the islands of the Pacific. The very first settlers were supplanted five hundred years later by migrants who arrived from Tahiti. And there was a further wave of migration, again from Tahiti, in the twelfth century. But after that, humans on Hawaii appear to have been pretty much on their own.

Life may well have been idyllic. There were wars between the six main inhabited islands, fearsome punishments handed out to enforce a rigid caste system, and human sacrifice performed as part of religious observance, none of which is to everyone's taste. But the benign climate, fertile land, abundant ocean and freedom from outside influence made for a simple and overwhelmingly pleasant life. Or so it seems, looking back.

What is undoubtedly the case is that, when it eventually came, contact with the outside world was a catastrophe for the Hawaiian people and their way of life.

Over-cooked

The great British explorer Captain James Cook discovered one or two of the Hawaiian islands in 1778 and received an extremely friendly reception. He returned in 1779 and landed for the first time on the largest of the islands. This island is the one called Hawaii but, since that is the name of the whole archipelago as well, it is generally known as the Big Island.

As every schoolboy knows, Captain Cook met his death in Hawaii, but I do not think that even as a schoolboy I had understood the extraordinary details of the events surrounding his demise.

On 17 January 1779 the Hawaiians were in the middle of a celebration of *makahiki,* a festival dedicated to their god of fertility, Lono. Legend had it that Lono, whose symbol was a white banner held high on a crossbow, would one day return, possibly to the bay known as Kealakekua, the pathway of the god. The legend said that he would arrive travelling clockwise round the island.

On that day in January Cook and his men – almost certainly the first outsiders these Hawaiians had ever seen – arrived in their two sailing ships, *Discovery* and *Resolution.* They dropped anchor in Kealakekua Bay, having first sailed clockwise round the island. The Hawaiians believed that Captain Cook was surely Lono made flesh. If there was any doubt about it, the white sails of his ships looked, to the Hawaiians, exactly like Lono's symbolic banners.

So, not surprisingly, Cook was hailed as a god. He was greeted by hundreds of canoes and thousands of people. The people bowed before him. He and his men were offered every comfort and entertainment.

The beautiful Hawaiian women were eager to enjoy the sexual favours of these divine visitors and, after months at sea, Cook's sailors really would have been super-human to have resisted them. They must have thought they had died and gone to heaven. As the song put it just under two centuries later, 'If paradise was half as nice as heaven that you take me to ...'

After two weeks, it was time to go. Cook had arrived as a god and was leaving with honour. But having set sail, things took a turn for the worse. A storm which broke the *Resolution's* mast forced Cook to return to the bay. This time there was no festival in progress, and his ships sailed the wrong way round the island. Gone were the crowds of adoring disciples. The natives were still friendly, but the broken mast had indicated a suspicious lack of godlike omnipotence. The Hawaiians started helping themselves to interesting artefacts on the ships, eventually making off with the *Discovery's* cutter.

Captain Cook knew what to do in these circumstances – he set off to take an important chief hostage in order to secure the cutter's return. Unfortunately, while he was doing this, there was a further altercation in which another, lesser, chief was killed.

This poisoned the atmosphere and, abandoning his hostage, Cook had to fight his way back towards his ship. The sailors fired at the Hawaiians, thinking that this would intimidate them in the same way that it had unnerved other Pacific islanders.

But it enraged them instead and, when Cook was struck on the head by a rock in the shallow waters of the bay, he was then stabbed to death in a frenzied attack, with many Hawaiian warriors passing the weapons between themselves to share in the kill. Cook's body was hacked to bits and taken away for some dreadful purpose. Most of it was returned, however, after Cook's distraught men took equally ferocious revenge on the Hawaiian people.

This violent end to Cook's glorious career marked the beginning of disaster for Hawaii. It was not, however, the violence which was Hawaii's doom. Friendly relations were restored more or less immediately once the remaining portions of Cook's body were handed back.

It was these friendly relations which caused the trouble. Cook had done his best to minimize intimate contact between his sailors and the alluring locals. Hawaiian women were not supposed to come onboard ship. Any of Cook's men known to be suffering from syphilis were to be thrashed if they slept with the local women. But in the way of these things, sexually transmitted diseases were transmitted sexually and they spread rapidly amongst the promiscuous islanders. Killing was done here, but with kindness.

For so long an isolated population, the Hawaiians had little resistance to venereal disease and the various other infections, plagues and pestilences that every group of visitors brought with them from civilization. In eighty years, their numbers fell from about 300 000 to fewer than 60 000.

In 1823, King Kamehameha II (Liholiho to his friends) and his favourite wife decided to go to Britain to visit King George IV. But before they could meet the King of England, both the King of Hawaii and his consort died of measles.

There were corresponding disasters to the fabric of the islands. At the time of Cook's discovery, Hawaii had extensive forests of sandalwood trees. The trees were bought by American shippers and sold to China where the wood was highly prized. But in fifty years the sandalwood was all gone and the profits mostly in the hands of the shippers. Kings and chiefs had been paid for the wood, but largely in expensive foreign imports. The ordinary Hawaiian had done back-breaking work hauling the wood to the coast, but a combination of *naïveté* and greed meant that very little was gained from what might have been a long-term money-spinner. Similarly, Hawaii came and went as a whaling centre as the whales came and went in the Pacific. Finally, sugar and then pineapples were developed as cash crops, with more and more labourers brought in from China and Japan to work in the fields.

Along the way, the Native Hawaiian population continued to decline and the number of incomers soared. The old Hawaiian religion of gods and taboos died away, and Christianity took its place. The ways of money, business and land-ownership so familiar in Europe and America supplanted the old feudal system and communal way of living which had applied before. The Hawaiian way of life withered away.

The Hawaii that Cook discovered was divided into its separate islands, but they were soon to be united under King Kamehameha the Great, who succeeded in imposing his rule on the other islands partially with the assistance of weaponry which he had acquired from Cook and later visitors.

The kings and queens who succeeded King Kamehameha were sometimes not so great but the Hawaiian monarchy lasted until 1894, when a consortium of *haole* (white) business people forced the establishment of a republic which four years later was annexed by the United States.

Hawaii had not been conquered by military action. The closest it had come to that had been in 1843 when Captain Lord George Paulet decided to claim Hawaii on behalf of Great Britain. He reckoned it was the sort of thing you were supposed to do in those days. Coming back from the South Seas without another piece of territory for the Empire would be like coming back from Torremolinos nowadays without a bullfight poster. But Queen Victoria was not amused to have a fellow royal family stripped of its domain and after six months Hawaii had to be given back to the Hawaiians.

Interestingly enough, the Union Jack forms part of the Hawaiian state flag, but not for any reasons connected with this very brief period as a

British possession. In fact, the Union Jack had already been included in Hawaii's flag some time before 1816, possibly because a British sea captain had given the nation one of his flags, perhaps in recognition of British protection at that time. There is also a fanciful story that the Hawaiian flag was deliberately made to look like a combination of the British Union Jack and the American Stars and Stripes in order to deter pirates from attacking Hawaiian shipping. If true, this could not have said much for the intelligence of the pirates.

There is the usual list of suspects for the bringing down of Hawaii as a nation state: plantation-owners, missionaries and the military.

The military were interested in Hawaii as a coaling station and strategic base. They anticipated that Pearl Harbor, the large natural haven just up the coast from Honolulu on the island of Oahu, would have an important part to play in some future war. The missionaries did their work in establishing the Christian faith in these far-off islands. And their descendants became important land-owners as the years went by. But it was the plantation-owners, businessmen and traders who did the most harm. They feared that Hawaii's last monarch, Queen Liliuokalani, was too keen to reassert the royal powers which they had prised from her predecessors. They wanted free access to American markets for their sugar. And so, despite a certain amount of discouragement from the American government of the day, Queen Liliuokalani was dethroned and she was replaced by a republic dominated by whites. The Queen was eventually convicted of treason, for daring to countenance resistance to the various land-owners and carpet-baggers who had assumed control of her kingdom. By 1959 Hawaii's Hawaiian history was all but forgotten and 90 per cent of its citizens voted in favour of it becoming an American state.

Fewer than 4 per cent of the population is of pure Hawaiian descent, and no more than 30 per cent claim to have any Hawaiian blood at all. Hawaii has become a true melting pot of Japanese, Caucasian, Chinese, Filipino, Puerto Rican and Polynesian ingredients. In the main it is an advertisement for inter-racial harmony but it does suggest that any idea of restoring a king of the Hawaiians would be difficult.

Aloha Athletic

Well, that was just the background. When I flew into the city of Honolulu which, together with Pearl Harbor and 80 per cent of the Hawaiian Islands' population is on the island of Oahu, I was wondering how we were going to capture the complex history and politics of Hawaii's situation. But the director had the problem well in hand – we were going to make a spoof of the TV series *Hawaii Five-O*.

I arrived in Honolulu on the evening of the day I had left Heathrow. Or it might have been the day before. Or possibly the day after. Hawaii is on the other side of the world from London, a few miles from the International Date Line as the Jumbo flies. By the time you get there you literally do not know what day of the week it is. All I did know was that I had to get up the next morning, very early, to be filmed rowing in a Hawaiian canoe because a canoe sequence is featured in the end credits of *Hawaii Five-0*.

A Hawaiian canoe is a long hollowed-out tree trunk, or nowadays an equivalent structure made from modern materials. It has an outrigger attached to one side to keep it from rolling over. The rowers sit in a line facing forwards. The oars are like large misshapen shovels which are used to propel the boat through the water. In my boat there were to be six oarsmen. Or, rather, five oarsmen and me.

The eclectic racial mix in Hawaii has produced some very beautiful people. Their coffee-coloured skin is enhanced by a life spent in the sun, and their muscles are toned by the outdoor life and healthy exercise.

On the other hand, my personal racial mixture is very British: Scots and English, with maybe a dash of Viking. My peelie-wally skin encases a body grown slack from a sedentary indoor life spent mainly under the grey skies of London. As a group we were not so much east meets west, as east meets etiolated.

ABOVE: *My first morning in Honolulu and I have to form part of a Hawaiian rowing squad. I am the third oarsman from the front.*
RIGHT: *Downtown Honolulu. American influence is just detectable.*

But off I set to make as big an idiot of myself as was absolutely necessary. The camera crew followed in a rather more comfortable, well-equipped, motor boat.

A strange thing happened just before we started. From nowhere a group of beautiful girls arrived. Possibly they were friends of the oarsmen, or of the captain of the motor boat. Maybe they just wanted a ride. More likely they were conforming to the ancient customary law of all nations which requires that all motor boats, pleasure craft and yachts sailing in or near fashionable resorts have to be decorated with an appropriate number of glamorous women. The next time you are in Monte Carlo, or the Caribbean, or Hawaii, check it out. Better still, get a boat.

The basics of rowing Hawaiian-style were reasonably easy to pick up. I do not think the technique is as efficient as the method used at Henley Regatta or in the Oxford and Cambridge Boat Race, but at least you can see where you are going and the novice has less chance of capsizing the whole boat by fouling his oar. You just toil away, pulling your shovel through the water, trying not to splash the guys sitting in front and behind. Alternate oarsmen row on opposite sides of the canoe: every ten or so strokes, on a signal from the lead man, you swap sides. We spent an hour or two rowing up and down in front of famous Honolulu landmarks. Sometimes putting on speed to catch a wave to surge towards the beach, sometimes stopping to rest or fool around jumping in and out of the clear, warm water. I did my best to keep paddle in time with the others, knowing that one false move would (a) slow us down and (b) inevitably be the only moment shown in the film.

Well, it was a small price to pay for being in such a glorious location. What is everyone on about? Hawaii seemed pretty good to me.

On the waterfront

You can see from the water, from the air and, for that matter, from any episode of *Hawaii Five-O,* that Honolulu has developed into a fully-fledged American city. It has high-rises and highways just like Miami or Los Angeles. So many Americans have come here to get away from it all that they have brought it all with them. Waikiki is a particular sadness to those who knew it in the old days. Waikiki is a narrow strip of land bordering the ocean, separated from the rest of Honolulu by a waterway called the Ala Wai Canal. More or less everything about it now is artificial. The canal is not a natural waterway, it is not even a canal for carrying barges. It was built in 1922, to drain the land that most of Waikiki is built on so that it could be developed as a resort. Waikiki does have a beautiful, if usually crowded, beach of white sand. But even that is not genuine any more – what with one thing and another, the original beach has been washed away so they have to go round the other islands digging up remote beaches to replace it. Now, that is obviously a sensible idea, because all Waikiki's hotels and souvenir shops have already been built so there would be no point in making the tourists traipse off to find these other beaches. Nowadays the mountain can be brought to Muhammad.

But for all that, Waikiki is good fun. Americans like shops and shopping, so there is a full range of expensive stores to keep them happy. And lots of cheap ones as well, which for some reason are all called ABC. Plus restaurants and bars and swimming pools. And it is just as well that there are things to do on land because there are so many hotel rooms in this tiny area that if everyone did go to the beach at the same time they would be rationed to one grain of sand each. As it is you can only get a tan if the person next to you has had their ears pierced.

There is a strong Japanese presence. They make up approximately 22 per cent of the population. Waikiki is also a popular Japanese tourist destination. Especially, it would seem, for weddings. Against a background of holiday-makers in bikinis and T-shirts, elaborately dressed Japanese couples pose for their wedding photographs in the grounds of the beach-front hotels. On the lawn of the Sheraton Moana Hotel I saw one wedding party, which included the bride in a perfect white dress and the groom sporting a matching white tail coat. In the shimmering heat they looked like figures from the top of a wedding cake designed by Liberace. This is all phoney. The couple will have got married already in some mundane ceremony in Japan, but then have flown to Hawaii for their honeymoon, during the course of which they stage a fantasy wedding for the photo album.

The Moana Surfrider hotel is a survivor from a golden and more elitist age of Waikiki holiday-making. A time when the Moana was one of only two or three hotels by the beach, and not part of an uninterrupted line of ocean-view balconies. It has been recently restored to what is known in the trade as its former glory. And in fact it is pretty glorious. In an elegant courtyard in the afternoon a group of Hawaiian musicians play steel guitars and sing their high-pitched whining songs which are strangely similar to Swiss yodels. This sort of stuff is played all over the place in Hawaii. On the radio, in the lifts, in restaurants and, in theory, it should get on your nerves. Yet, rather like bagpipes, it has such an emotional haunting quality that you can listen to it for days on end before screaming for it to stop.

The group in this high-class hotel are very good and they are accompanied by two beautiful girls waving their hips in sensuous hula dances. Hawaiian girls look almost too beautiful. A perfection of tan-coloured skin, curvaceous figures, long black hair and permanently smiling lips. Perhaps they are not real either. But if you can think of no better accompaniment to a full afternoon tea (choice of various Twinings teas made at your table, scones and cakes), I suggest you go there.

We will fight them on the beaches

We started our serious filming on a less artificial beach at Makapuu, a few miles east of Honolulu. For a year or so this was the site of a beach occupation. Native Hawaiians had built a veritable shanty town of tents and shelters around what is a holy place in Hawaiian tradition, but which in the modern world is supposed to be a public beach where you are not allowed to stay overnight.

On the beach I spoke to A'O Pohaku. She is a leader of one of the many organizations pressing for Hawaiian sovereignty. She believes that it is necessary for the spirituality of the Hawaiian people to be retained, spirituality being the element which is most notably lacking in the American consumer society which currently holds sway here as in so much of the rest of the world. Even after all the shacks had been removed, A'O and her supporters had been coming back to the beach to water the plants they had put around a stone cairn marking a spot significant to their ancient beliefs.

For all the spiritual aspects of the movement, and an aspiration for sovereignty, there was also a more immediate, practical aim to the beach protest.

Native Hawaiians have felt themselves marginalized by Hawaiian society as it has developed over the last hundred years. Rather like Aborigines in Australia, they have become strangers in their own land. They claim to feature higher in levels of unemployment and homelessness than all other racial groups. Their culture was deliberately suppressed. The Japanese and the Chinese and, of course, the Americans were allowed to have schools which taught in their own language, but not the Hawaiians who were living here before anyone else.

They are now fighting back and using the law to do it. Again like the Aborigines in Australia, and Indian tribes in America, they are using ancient treaties and statutes to support their claim for title to land. In 1848 there was a fundamental distribution of land in Hawaii under King Kamehameha III. Roughly one-third of Hawaiian land was to be

TOP: *A'O Pohaku explains the spiritual significance of the sacred site of the beach occupation at Makapuu.* ABOVE: *Dennis 'Bumpy' Kanahele, a Hawaiian leader to be reckoned with.*

kept by the king, one-third was to go to chiefs and one-third was to be government land for the Native Hawaiian people who, even then, were already heavily outnumbered by newcomers.

Most of the Crown land and the government land was later ceded to the United States government, but Native Hawaiians have insisted that it was done without their consent and some of this land has been returned to Hawaiians so they can establish homesteads for the homeless. The beach occupation was intended to force the relevant government department to allocate some of this land to the occupiers. In that it has succeeded, and a chunk of land has been handed over. You can see this either as squatters jumping the (long) queue for the allocation of homestead land, or the first step towards the reassertion of Hawaiian rights.

On the newly allocated land up in the hills I met the leader of the occupation, Dennis 'Bumpy' Kanahele. Pure Hawaiians tend to be large people, and Bumpy looks every inch, or rather every cubic inch, a Hawaiian leader. He had been described to me as a bit of a bully, liable to intimidate his opponents with his sheer physical presence. But with me he was all smiles and amiability. When I jokingly offered to arm-wrestle with him as we sat chatting at a table he kindly refrained from snapping my hand off at the wrist. He and his people were busy building an encampment to live in. There was a communal dining area under a tent and any number of subsidiary shacks and vehicles around which people were sawing wood and chopping down trees in what I assume was an organized way. The trees they were felling were eucalyptus trees which, not being native to Hawaii, they regarded as something that should be removed.

Bumpy makes an obviously charismatic rebel leader. Apart from anything else, the thing which hampers him and the rest of the sovereignty movement is the low numbers of Native Hawaiians and the high number of sovereignty groups. Like all radical movements, there is much scope for arguments about to what extent one should co-operate with the powers-that-be, and even more scope for personality clashes. Bumpy scores highly on personality and on the fact that he dares to confront the authorities, but he is condemned by some for negotiating the grant of the land. But on the homestead, Bumpy was king and monarch of all the ground they were surveying.

Yet it seemed to me that the whole movement was at least one hundred years too late. It is unlikely that the majority of the population now resident on Hawaii would want to break links with America and, even if they did, would the 70 per cent of the population who have no

Hawaiian blood be prepared to hand over any more power to those who do? To the modern way of thinking, the very notion of determining a person's rights by reference to his racial origin looks weird, if not positively immoral. But the law in Hawaii has already adopted that approach. Positive discrimination is exercised in favour of people who can prove they have 50 per cent or more Native Hawaiian blood.

Pay paradise

Hawaiian life of a sort is preserved every night at Paradise Cove along the coast. This is beach-side entertainment purporting to provide a genuine Hawaiian evening. Coach parties are bussed there for a bit of a knees-up. Drop-dead gorgeous girls in grass skirts and coconut-shell bras pose with you for photographs. Later they dance and cheer as their male counterparts shin up trees or organize the punters into Hawaiian activities. Old Hawaiian sports on the sand are played by old American sports in the crowd. The accent is on family fun. There is plenty to eat and drink and songs and laughter as night falls. The whole evening might not be to your taste, however, especially if you have any taste. It is a shame to see a native culture reduced to a series of catchpenny attractions, but who can doubt that this sort of thing would be here whether Hawaii was part of the United States or was an independent nation trying to attract American dollars for its balance of trade?

Sorry seems to be the hardest word

In 1993 the United States actually apologized to Native Hawaiians for the overthrowing of their kingdom. Public Law 103-150 is a resolution of the Senate and House of Representatives which in three or four pages sets out the history of America's illegal take-over and then apologizes for it.

It is quite an abject admission of wrong-doing. Its only concession to *realpolitik* is to add a one-line disclaimer which says that nothing in the Resolution 'is intended as a settlement of any claims against the United States'.

As Bumpy was keen to point out, it is all very well for America to apologize for illegally taking the country. But surely they must give it back? A thief who says sorry for taking your car does not usually get to keep it.

Well, deciding the sovereignty of a country is not as straightforward as determining the ownership of personal property. But America's

apology, which was probably put through in fulfilment of a presidential election promise, certainly opens up a can of worms. And the man to use the worms to full advantage is Hayden Burgess.

Hayden Burgess lives about 30 or 40 miles out of Honolulu in a pleasant, if slightly run-down suburb which he said was occupied in large part by Native Hawaiians. It looks very American for all that, with quiet streets of green grass verges and neat houses. At the side of Hayden's house are a couple of wooden prefabs, one of which he has converted into his office. From here he runs his legal practice which is focused on arguing in favour of the rights of Native Hawaiians.

ABOVE AND RIGHT: *On my visit to Paradise Cove, I joined in the family fun and had the parrots lying in my hands.*

Once upon a time Hayden served in the American military but he got booted out when, after becoming conscious of his Hawaiian identity, he refused to salute the Stars and Stripes. He continues with what is basically a conscientious objection to everything to do with the American presence in Hawaii with all the zeal of an obsessive combined with all the tenacity of a lawyer. Plus, it should be noted, an enormous amount of charm.

He refuses to accept American citizenship, which means he declines to have a Social Security number. This makes many aspects of life rather difficult. He cannot, of course, pay taxes or apply for a driving licence, or comply with a hundred and one other requirements of the state and its bureaucracy.

In a more intolerant age or place Hayden would have been thrown into jail years ago but the way things are in America he is free to practise at the Honolulu Bar and argue cases in front of judges whose legitimacy he utterly denies. His logic is faultless. The American take-over was illegal. Congress has admitted that, in Public Law 103-150. Therefore everything which flows from that take-over is illegal. All title to land granted under American laws, all state structures, all agencies. Everything.

If the whole issue is ever decided in the courtroom you feel Hayden could get a result for Hawaii. He is convinced that he has right on his side and that it will see him through to victory, even though his land has been taken from him. Possession may be nine parts of the law, but self-possession is nine parts of the lawyer.

To say the least, there are a few problems with this approach. Most territory around the world has at some time in the past been won by right of conquest, the usual term for trespass and larceny on a grand scale. Should all conquests be subject to legal analysis, generations after they were committed? And what about immigrants who have arrived since the unlawful events that are being complained of? And anyway, was the manoeuvring for power in Hawaii really as bad as armed conquest?

There are a number of different ways forward for Hawaiian nationalists. The restoration of the sovereign state of Hawaii, coupled with the return of its monarchy, is the most extreme possibility. There could be independence without the monarchy, or the setting up of a sovereign nation with the United States, based on the model of several mainland Native American peoples. Some people would settle for little more than the setting aside of sort of Hawaiian reservations in the islands to reflect their historic demands. Only the future will tell if history can be rewritten in some way.

For the present, Hayden lives his life in as Hawaiian a way as possible. He prefers to be known by his Hawaiian name of Poka Laenui. He grows only native species of plants in his garden, and raises edible freshwater fish in a tank in his backyard. The tank is a high-tech structure with pumps and filters, but it follows the Hawaiian tradition of growing fish for the table in fish ponds. He will be demanding road signs in Welsh next.

American pie

On the way back to downtown Honolulu we visited a more up-market suburb to hear the views of two other Hawaiians. The suburb of Makiki is a part of town built on a hill overlooking the skyscrapers of Honolulu central. Dr Esau Masunga has a house there. He is a second-generation Hawaiian, a dentist of Japanese extraction. He sees no prospect of Hawaii breaking away from America. Nor can his friend Lloyd Jones, also a Hawaiian citizen but originally from Australia. They point out that people like them have as much right to a say in Hawaiian affairs as anybody of the original Hawaiian race. And their life here is based on Hawaii as an American state. As it is they can travel to and from the other forty-nine states, their children can attend the American university of their choice. They do not need a visa to visit, or live in, California. And they are not about to vote any of that away.

Even more forthright in his criticism of the Hawaiian cause was Bob Parkinson who we visited later in his apartment overlooking the Ala Wai Canal. He is in real estate and thinks the Hawaiians should join the real world. He is impatient with Native Hawaiians sitting around demanding compensation or hand-outs because of injustices that may have been suffered by their grandfathers. It is all in the past. It is tough luck they lost their kingdom. Sure, it may have been wrong then, but now they should just knuckle down, get a job, get a life and stop living off welfare. He thinks it is only the dead hand of political correctness which prevents people speaking out in praise of all the benefits which flow from the connection with America and against all this Native Hawaiian nonsense.

I tried to persuade him that an independent Hawaii could turn itself into great offshore tax haven. I think he was interested, but it was not quite enough to bring him round.

OVERLEAF: *Work, work, work – discussing the preservation of Hawaiian culture with one of the performers at Paradise Cove.*

We were off to another apartment. In the opening sequence of *Hawaii Five-0,* Jack Lord (who played Steve McGarrett) stands on a balcony overlooking the city of Honolulu, a rose-white city half as old as Los Angeles. So we were going to re-create that sequence with me in the Jack Lord role. In fact, in an unusual and somewhat pointless piece of honesty in film-making, I was to stand on the balcony they had actually used. Apparently the flat really had been owned by the actor Jack Lord.

It is a penthouse and the balcony consists of a large flat roof. Luckily for us the flat was for sale and so we were able to get permission to film there. To re-create the shot we had to hire a helicopter to hover above the rooftops so the camera could catch me executing a dynamic turn and resembling the lantern-jawed crime fighter. I stood on the roof as the Swiss pilot drifted towards me. (I don't know what a Swiss was doing in Hawaii. Perhaps he had been attracted there by the yodelling music.) I had to make my move only when the helicopter got as close as possible, my cue coming from a shout relayed on a walkie-talkie by my feet. In the event, I could not hear anything but the noise of the chopper's engine so I had to guess when to go. I did not want to move too soon but, if I went too late, instead of *Hawaii Five-O* we would have re-created a bit of *Catch 22.* You know, the scene when the helicopter cuts someone's body in half.

Once we had finished, the real estate agent tried to interest me in buying the apartment. Apparently, $2 000 000 gets you an attractive service flat with three bedrooms. In addition to the $2 000 000, you have to pay $700 a month for maintenance charges and $515 a month property tax. An ideal holiday home for a TV star, the agent thought. Something tells me that TV pays better in the US than it does in the UK.

Cook's tour

It was time to pay a visit to the Big Island of Hawaii. For this we flew the 200 miles or so to land at the pleasant outdoor airport of Keahole-Kona while our all luggage flew in the opposite direction to Kauai, the island at the opposite end of the chain of islands. It really boosts your faith in airline security to know that twenty metal boxes of camera equipment can fly unaccompanied in a small plane.

Would we be forced to take some time off while we waited in a luxury hotel for our camera to catch up with us? No such luck – it turned up early next morning.

The country of Hawaii is rather bigger than I thought. It had been possible to spend hours driving on the freeways leading out of Honolulu without running out of road. The total land area of the islands is some-thing like 6400 square miles, which is eight times the size of Wales. The Big Island, 96 miles long and 76 miles wide, is much bigger than all of the other islands put together. But as if concerned to maintain its largest island status, the Big Island continues to grow, its shoreline pushed outwards by lava flows which leak from its periodically active volcanoes.

Paradise in paradise

The luxury hotel complex we were visiting was the Hilton Waikoloa. And I do mean luxury, and I do mean complex. This awesome hotel development, which in its brief history was once a Hyatt Regency, has more than 1200 rooms and covers 62 acres of land. To get there, the road from the airport goes through barren countryside which is a moonscape of black volcanic rocks only slowly being colonized here and there by the hardiest of plants.

Once you get to the hotel you can forget barren. The approach roads are bordered by strips of verdant grass verges and a neat row of trees watered by automatic sprinklers. To the horizon there is a view of bleak, black rocks which will take years, centuries maybe, to turn into fertile ground. But the foreground is a green and pleasant band put there for your delight. Herbaceous window-dressing, it prepares you for the pleasures inside the resort. For, once inside, there is everything that your heart, stomach and most other parts of your body could desire. There are seven restaurants serving food from Italy, Japan, America, France, and even Polynesia. There are shops, swimming pools, salt-water lagoons, golf courses, bars and $4 million worth of art.

To get around the resort you can use the train service. The trains stop in the enormous open-air lobby and take you to the tower which houses your bedroom or away to whichever restaurant happens to take your fancy. If you think that travelling on this American equivalent of the Docklands Light Railway lacks romance, there is an alternative canal service featuring little boats captained by smart young things in jaunty yachting outfits.

In the sea-water lagoon you can swim and interact with dolphins. I was rather keen to do this but all three female dolphins were pregnant at the time and so not up to appearing on-camera. And the male, I assume, was too exhausted.

Waikiki may be artificial but it has nothing on this place. Hawaii is famous for its waterfalls, but there is no need to go looking for them around the islands because a few of them have been created within this

LEFT: *A paradise within a paradise, one of the artificial waterfalls in the Hilton Waikoloa, Big Island.* ABOVE: *Moani Akaka of the Office of Hawaiian Affairs and I sailed around the canal transportation system at the resort and wondered if all this luxury could be justified.*

resort. Just like the real thing, if you ignore the sound of the water being pumped back up to the top of the rock. There are trees aplenty, all of which were shipped here at vast expense. A million cubic yards of topsoil was delivered in lorry-loads from the mountains; the canal boats, designed by Disney, were flown in from Florida; the trains came from Switzerland.

This is excess taken to excess, comfort at a level which is quite discomforting. Don't get me wrong. It is all highly enjoyable, but a bit weird, soulless and definitely lacking in the spirituality that A'O had been talking about. You can sit on a beach here, but not only is the sand imported, it is enclosed in a man-made lagoon and faces away from the sea. The sea does wash up against the nearby shore, but the coastline is made up of hard, scratchy rocks. And you do not come here for anything hard or scratchy. There is no awe to be experienced at the wonders of nature, only wonder at the power of money.

Perhaps this is the true meaning of paradise? Although we generally use the word to mean the Garden of Eden before the Fall or as a synonym for Heaven, originally in Persia a paradise was simply a pleasure garden, a place set apart to be enjoyed by those escaping from the awfulness of life. And this is a pleasure garden where there are no poor people, no muggers, beggars or street entertainers. Only employees of Hilton International. A true paradise, in fact. Either that, or a re-creation of *The Prisoner*.

Just one thing. In paradise, however you define it, do you really want to find yourself dashing from the lift to catch the train on your way to dinner?

We filmed an interview with Moani Akaka as she and I sailed on one of the boats on the canal. She is another Hawaiian activist, but one who has agreed to become a trustee of the state-sponsored Office of Hawaiian Affairs. She had never been to the resort before and rather disapproved of it. She had specific complaints about the alteration to the coastline which had been made when the complex was built and about the resources that the resort consumes. She was also concerned about the wages structure and the distance that employees have to travel to work there.

Anything so new and so luxurious does look rather tasteless built amidst the poverty of its surroundings, but the land that the resort is built on is barren rock. Its only assets are sun and sea, both of which are effectively exploited by what is essentially a giant tourist farm. OK, so the tourists are not free-range but, if they like being penned up in this pleasure factory, what harm is being done?

Moani Akaka retained her doubts as we sailed along in the heat of the day. As we went up and down the canal we realized that the boats are attached to a mono-rail under the water. The guys in nautical uniforms are not really sailing them from landing stage to landing stage – they only control the speed as they go along their fixed course. The whole thing is a train with the right kind of water on the line. Even the canal boats are not really real.

Once more on to the beach

Back in what we assumed was the real world, we went to see Maloni Pai who was at the centre of another beach protest. Pai and his family live on a beach which actually comes under the jurisdiction of the National Park Service. They do not hold formal title to the place, but claim that because Pai's family have lived there for generations they have an ancient right to remain.

The family live in a series of lightweight structures and shacks right by the water's edge. This is the traditional Hawaiian way, though they do have generators for electricity and large pick-up trucks for transport. Pai's own house is on a little island, a tiny circle of sand like the ones that cartoonists put shipwrecked sailors on. Except that this is not surrounded by miles of ocean, it is only a few yards from the shore.

Pai is a rather intense man, anxious to preserve or recapture the ways of his ancestors. Before we begin the interview he insists on saying a prayer to his gods at a special shrine. This resembles a bamboo scaffolding tower, but its various parts have a significance in the worship of the various ancient Hawaiian deities. It is sited on a particular piece of rocky shoreline. Pai warned us not approach too close to the shrine unless our intentions were good. 'Harm awaits anyone who goes beyond this rock, unless his heart is pure', he solemnly informed us. Superstitious nonsense, of course, but on going beyond the rock, the director stumbled clumsily and cut his leg open on the sharp coral.

Pai wants to stay here to look after the beach. The Park Service want him to go because this is a heritage site, and he and his structures are messy and his dogs are dangerous. Pai argues that he is the heritage and belongs here. He reckons enough damage has been done to this area already. In one direction there is a yachting marina, and further up the beach *haole* nudists come and display their bodies in a way the white man used to preach was sinful. Pai has set up a school here to teach the Hawaiian language and customs. We were going to film it, but the only pupils that day were his uncle and aunt.

ABOVE AND RIGHT: *Maloni Pai is determined to live on the beach against the wishes of the National Park Service. The ceremonial robes he wears for television interviews.*

How genuine is this slice of Old Hawaii? When I interviewed him Pai was dressed in a loin cloth and ochre robes. This is what a Hawaiian should look like and how he wished to appear on-camera. But before and afterwards he was in a T-shirt and shorts like any other American citizen.

In memoriam

There is a memorial to Captain Cook right by the spot where he was hacked to death in Kealakekua Bay over 200 years ago. It is quite easy to reach it by boat. The film was to start with me arriving there by helicopter, but we actually got to it by going overland. And to do that you

have to be ready for a rough journey and to know where you are going. There is no sign pointing the way to the memorial at the point where you have to turn off the main road. There is only the roughest of tracks leading first through brush and woodland and then over volcanic rock. You can drive part of the way but eventually you have to get out of your vehicle and walk the last mile or so. When you finally get there the memorial is a simple white obelisk surrounded by a chain fence. It is decorated with badges and symbols of ships whose sailors have made the pilgrimage to the site. Its closeness to the place where Cook was actually put to death, and its remoteness from pretty well everything else, gives it the poignance of a grave accidentally discovered on a lonely hillside.

The lack of exploitation of the place as a tourist attraction suggests that Hawaiians are not that interested in the British explorer who literally put them on the map. There is something positively un-American about the lack of refreshment facilities of any sort. Perhaps this is a corner of a foreign field which does remain forever England.

Independence days

We did not remain on the Big Island much longer. We had to get back to Oahu for the 100th anniversary of Hawaii's last day as an independent kingdom on 3 July. There was to be a march through Waikiki in commemoration, and as part of the continuing campaign for Hawaiian rights.

Most of the sovereignty campaigners I had met in Hawaii were taking part. Hayden Burgess made a speech to the crowd at the start of the march. As ever, he was sticking to his principles. Permission to stage this march had not been sought from the occupying powers-that-be, because they had no right to be in power. Not even the City of Honolulu Traffic Department.

But having got wind of it all, the police had asked them to march on the pavement and not the roadway itself. A request that Hayden was going to ignore. A Hawaiian should always be able to walk down a Hawaiian road if he wanted to do. Certainly that was what Hayden himself was going to do, and he suggested everyone else followed suit. So off went the march, with everyone daring to stay off the sidewalk and remain in the gutter. There were about 1500 marchers from a variety of independence groups, plus a bishop in a flowery shirt, gay rights activists, environmentalists, anarchists and royalists. The rainbow alliance of the sort of people who like to go on demos. They walked along the road but the police did not seem to mind. They marched past loitering tourists out taking the evening air but the tourists did not seem to care. None of the tourists I spoke to opposed the idea of Hawaiian independence, and that cannot just have been because Bumpy was somewhere looking on. It was a pleasant evening's stroll the length of central Waikiki, drawing the attention of anyone who wanted to listen to the grievances of the Hawaiians. It was all very peaceful and unthreatening. At the end everyone got into cars or buses and went home.

The next day was 4 July and at Schofield Military Base there were celebrations for America's Independence Day. I thought this might feature an awesome display of America's military presence and power. But in fact it was more of a family day out for the soldiers and their families. Between 40 000 and 50 000 people were scattered over a large field eating and drinking and enjoying the all-American fun. There were hamburgers and hot dogs and a parachute display team. A brass band played the 1812 Overture. At nightfall there were fireworks on a grand scale. Before that a famous singer called Wayne Newton had flown in from Las Vegas with his orchestra to belt out a selection of hits, standards and patriotic songs to entertain the troops.

Even here I could find almost nobody in the crowds of GIs to say that America should hang on to Hawaii at all costs or even hang on to it at all, though I must admit I was not able to speak to Wayne Newton about it. So, unlikely as it first seemed, maybe Hawaii will be the last star on, first star off the American flag, as somebody's T-shirt had said on the march through Waikiki.

Take me to your leader

Before leaving Hawaii I met the State Governor, John D. Waihee III. He saw me in a proper American press-call room. There were rows of chairs for the media, a lectern with insignia on it and a desk for the Governor. He was happy to talk about the sovereignty issue. He is part-Hawaiian himself and reckons that there will be some sort of autonomy for Hawaiians in the near future. He expressed, in very ambiguous terms, his support for the independence movement, though he came across as a very American-style politician.

But if Hawaii were to become a monarchy again, who would be king? Not John D. Waihee III. King Kamehameha VI is the answer, but where is he to be found? Sadly, the answer is in a Federal prison in Colorado.

King Kamehameha, or Windy Lorenzo, was sentenced to thirty-three months in prison for an attempted tax fraud. It was a rather complicated crime. Windy had been elected king by a council of chiefs which had considered his genealogy, fitness to rule and so on. He had then laid claim to large tracts of Crown lands and billed the present occupiers for rent of $750 000. When that was not paid he applied for a refund on the tax he would have paid on that money, had he received it. As an assertion of royal power it seems rather confused. As a crime it was bound to be detected as he was asking the Inland Revenue to repay money he had not paid out in the first place. So he was rather easily caught. Colorado is a long way from Hawaii, but apparently there is a no Federal jail in Hawaii.

So on the way home to London we stopped off at Denver and went over to interview King Windy. It looks as though Colorado has been selected as the prison which is about as far away in miles and spirit as you could get from Hawaii to incarcerate the pretender to the Hawaiian throne. I assumed it was a deliberate policy, but the truth may be more mundane.

Los Angeles and San Francisco have Federal prisons but they are full of drug dealers and the like. The inland state of Colorado actually built a new prison and donated it to the Federal authorities, not to deal with

ABOVE: *The Cook memorial on the Big Island.* RIGHT: *Yankee Doodle Dandy, fourth of July celebrations at Schofield military base.*

local crime but to provide local employment opportunities for prison guards and so on. And prisoners from all over the country are transferred there to use the available prison cells.

It is a smart high-tech clean-cut kind of place set on a bleak Colorado hillside. A maximum-security institution is being built alongside it, but the prison Windy is in has fairly low-key security. For most of the prisoners, it would be a long way home from here, and most of them are not the type to try to make it. We received every co-operation from the authorities to film in and around the prison, including filming an interview with Windy himself.

Whatever the reason for his being there, and however up-to-date the facilities, Windy is not enjoying his time in custody. He claims he was set up by the IRS in the first place and does not see why he should be punished. He has lost a lot of weight, the food is not to his taste and he fears the whole institution may be polluted with radioactivity. He is filled with a sense of injustice at the overthrow of what should now be

his kingdom and will continue to work towards the restoration of the monarchy when he gets out of gaol. Like all the activists I spoke to back in Hawaii, he fails to explain how the monarchy could be restored if the majority of the people now living in the islands do not want it.

He is a long way from home and a long way from being in power. For Windy to become king of a fully independent nation of Hawaii he would need the support of the majority of all the people of Hawaii and the acquiescence of the American government. The last time anybody attempted to cede from the Union it lead to civil war. And the only good thing to come from that was *Gone with the Wind*. Perhaps Windy will have better luck. I think he is going to need it.

BIBLIOGRAPHY

OUR MAN IN GOA

Crowther, G. and Finlay, H. *India* Lonely Planet Publications, 1993.

Fish, Curry and Rice, A Citizen's Report on the Goan Environment Ecoforum.

Hall, M. *A Window on Goa* Quiller Press, 1994.

Richards, J.M. *Goa* C. Hurst, 1981.

Shales, M. *The Footloose Guide to Southern India and Goa* Simon & Schuster, 1992.

OUR MAN IN HAVANA

Calder, S. and Hatchwell, E. *Travellers' Survival Kit CUBA* Vacation Work, 1993.

Cameron, S. and Box, B. *Caribbean Islands Handbook* Trade & Travel, 1994.

Rius, *Cuba for Beginners* Pathfinder, 1986.

Greene, G. *Our Man in Havana* Penguin, 1971.

Horowitz, I. *The Conscience of Worms and the Cowardice of Lions* Transaction, U.S., 1993.

Murray, M. (interview with Ricardo Alarcón), *Cuba and the United States* Ocean Press, 1993.

Murray, M. *Cruel and Unusual Punishment* Ocean Press, 1993.

Fundacion Magazine, Summer 1993 Cuban American National Association

OUR MAN IN THE MAASAI MARA

Finlay, H. and Crowther, G. *Kenya* Lonely Planet Publications, 1994.

Beckwith, C. *Masai* Harvill, 1991.

Trillo, R. *Kenya, the Rough Guide* Rough Guides, 1993.

OUR MAN IN DOMINICA

Cameron, S. and Box, B. *Caribbean Islands Handbook* Trade and Travel, 1994.

Evans, P.C.H. *Dominica: Nature Island of the Caribbean* Hansib, 1989.

Higbie, J. *Eugenia* Macmillan, 1992.

Honychurch L, *Dominica Isle of Adventure* Macmillan, 1991.

Thomson, R. *Green Gold* Latin America Bureau, 1987.

OUR MAN IN THE TIMBERLANDS

Foreman, D. and Haywood, B. *Ecodefense* Abbzug Press, U.S., 1993.

Seidman, D. *Showdown at Opal Creek* Carroll & Graf, U.S., 1993.

Warren, S. and Long-Ishikawa, T. *Oregon Handbook* Moon Publications, U.S., 1994.

OUR MAN IN HAWAII

Bendure, G. and Friary, N. *Hawaii, Travel Survival Kit* Lonely Planet Publications, 1993.

Hoffer, H.J. *Insight Guides: Hawaii* APA Publications, 1988.

Queen Liliuokalani, *Hawaii's Story by Hawaii's Queen,* C.E.Tuttle, U.S., 1976.

INDEX